MERCY AND THE BIBLE

MERCY AND THE BIBLE

WHY IT MATTERS!

RONALD D. WITHERUP, PSS

Paulist Press
New York / Mahwah, NJ

Material in this book has been updated and expanded from articles previously published by *The Pastoral Review*: serving the Church since 1931. Reproduced with permission of the Publisher. http://www.thepastoralreview.org. This permission covers the following articles:
"The Year of Mercy," July–Aug 2015, vol. 11, no. 4.
"Mercy in the Old Testament," Sept–Oct 2015, vol. 11, no. 5.
"Mercy in the Teaching of Jesus," Nov–Dec 2015, vol. 11, no. 6.
"Luke, the Gospel of Mercy," Jan–Feb 2016, vol. 12, no. 1.
"Mercy in the Letters of Paul," Mar–April 2016, vol. 12, no. 2.
"St Paul Revisited," July–Aug 2016, vol. 12, no. 4.

Jacket image: James J. Tissot, "The Return of the Prodigal Son" (1886–1994). Online Collection of Brooklyn Museum and is considered to have no known copyright restrictions. Used with permission.
Jacket and book design by Lynn Else

Library of Congress Cataloging-in-Publication Data
Names: Witherup, Ronald D., 1950– author.
Title: Mercy and the Bible : why it matters! / Ronald D. Witherup, P.S.S.
Description: New York : Paulist Press, 2018. | Includes bibliographical references.
Identifiers: LCCN 2017058864 (print) | LCCN 2018022994 (ebook) | ISBN 9781587687525 (ebook) | ISBN 9780809106516 (hardcover : alk. paper)
Subjects: LCSH: God (Christianity)—Mercy. | Mercy—Biblical teaching. | Catholic Church—Doctrines.
Classification: LCC BT153.M4 (ebook) | LCC BT153.M4 W58 2018 (print) | DDC 241/.4—dc23
LC record available at https://lccn.loc.gov/2017058864

ISBN 978-0-8091-0651-6 (hardcover)
ISBN 978-1-58768-752-5 (e-book)

Published by Paulist Press
997 Macarthur Boulevard
Mahwah, New Jersey 07430

www.paulistpress.com

Printed and bound in the
United States of America

For Pope Francis
In gratitude for his prophetic call
for a more merciful Church

CONTENTS

ACKNOWLEDGMENTS

This book began to take shape during the Year of Mercy (December 8, 2015 to November 20, 2016) proclaimed by Pope Francis. Most of the chapters are revised and expanded articles that were originally published as a series in *The Pastoral Review*, a British journal aimed at informing priests, deacons, catechists, and educated laypeople of current issues in Bible and theology. I am grateful to the editor, the late Father Michael A. Hayes (1957–2017); the editorial administrator, Ms. Stephanie Bennett; and the publisher, Mr. Ignatius Kusiak, for their kind permission to republish these articles in an updated and expanded format.

In addition, I have added an introduction and a closing chapter to round out the theme, as well as introduced reflection questions and a few recommendations for further reading. I hope these resources will prove stimulating for those who might wish to pursue the theme in more depth. They also might aid those who use the book for group discussion. Given the intended audience, notes have been kept to an absolute minimum, but the author gratefully acknowledges the contributions of many scholars who have written about the theme of mercy and provided important background material.

As always, I recommend that readers wanting to get the most out of these reflections consult their Bible for reference. The best way to learn from the Bible is to read it. While I cite essential passages to illustrate my arguments, consulting the full biblical context will make the effort of reading this book more productive.

I am also grateful to Professor John R. Donahue, SJ, who not only carefully read the manuscript and functioned as the *censor librorum*, but who also provided several helpful references, and to the Very Rev. John C. Kemper, PSS, provincial of the U.S. Province of Sulpicians for granting permission to publish this book. Of course, any errors that remain are my own.

In addition, I express sincere thanks to Paulist Press, especially to Rev. Mark-David Janus, president and publisher, and Paul McMahon, my editor, for their assistance. The entire staff of Paulist Press has done excellent work in producing this book, and I am grateful for their professionalism and confidence.

Ronald D. Witherup
Solemnity of the Annunciation

INTRODUCTION

On March 13, 2015, when Pope Francis announced the extraordinary jubilee "Year of Mercy," which ran from December 8, 2015 (Solemnity of the Immaculate Conception and the fiftieth anniversary of the closing of the Second Vatican Council) to November 20, 2016 (Solemnity of Christ the King), one might have heard a collective groan, especially among clergy. What to make of another "themed" year?

The fact is that recent popes, from Saint John Paul II (1920–2005) to Benedict XVI (b. 1927) to Pope Francis (b. 1936), have declared an unprecedented number of "holy years" or years with special themes. Saint John Paul II, in particular, was concerned to orient the Church and the world at large toward a major milestone in the history of Christianity, the third Christian millennium, which began in 2000. Thus, he organized a series of themed years to build up to that epic point and to carry the Church into the first decade of the new millennium. His 1994 apostolic letter *Tertio Millennio Adviente* ("As the Third Millennium Approaches") called for a preparatory period of three years, each with a specific trinitarian theme. Thus, 1997 was the year devoted to the Son, Jesus Christ, 1998 to the Holy Spirit, and 1999 to the Father. The theme of the Jubilee Year 2000 itself was "Christ Yesterday, Today, and Tomorrow." It was based upon a biblical affirmation from the Letter to the

Hebrews: "Jesus Christ is the same yesterday and today and forever" (Heb 13:8).

During each of these holy years, many thousands of pilgrims came to Rome to participate in multiple events throughout the year, some of them associated with specific groups of pilgrims (priests, religious women and men, seminarians, deacons, etc.) and others associated with various religious ceremonies, such as canonizations. The scope was truly grandiose, worthy of crossing the threshold of the new Christian millennium. The pope officially closed the jubilee year 2000 on the Solemnity of the Epiphany (January 6, 2001) and issued a closing document, *Novo Millennio Ineunte* ("Upon Entering the Millennium") that outlined his vision for the Church's future.

Despite appearances, holy years are not a modern invention. The idea of a jubilee year is, in fact, a biblical notion. The word *jubilee* comes from the Hebrew *yobel*, referring to a ram's horn that was fashioned into a musical instrument (the *shofar*, which the Latin Vulgate translates with *tuba*) used especially in liturgical rituals. Even today, synagogues use the shofar for special feasts like Rosh Hashanah (the Jewish new year) or Yom Kippur (the day of atonement, the holiest feast in the Jewish calendar, which brings to a climax the ten-day celebration of the Jewish new year). One might almost visualize, for example, a ceremony that is alluded to in a passage from the prophet Joel, which is read at the beginning of the Christian season of Lent: "Blow the trumpet in Zion; proclaim a fast; call a holy assembly" (Joel 2:15, au. trans.).

A jubilee year came at the end of a cycle of forty-nine years (seven periods of seven years; seven being a symbolic number of perfection). It was thus the fiftieth year, intended to allow for new beginnings. The practice is described at length in the Old Testament in the Book of Leviticus (see 25:8–17, 23–55; 27:16–25). The idea is a cycle of six years followed by a seventh "sabbatical year," recalling the model established in Genesis at Creation, when God rested on the seventh day, the sabbath, after six days of work creating the universe (Gen 2:2). At the end of seven periods of this cycle came the jubilee year, when the land was to be returned to its ancestral owners, and the fields that had been farmed were to be left fallow so that they could recover their fertility. In addition, slaves were to be set free during the jubilee year. The entire year was to be an occasion for new beginnings, a kind of new creation to "set things right." It was a way to give hope to the poor that they could eventually have a fresh start in life and would not need to be forever stuck in their unfortunate circumstances. While scholars have raised some questions about how literally all the aspects of the jubilee year were enacted, there is little doubt that the concept was an important part of Israelite festivals and liturgical feasts.

Christian jubilee (or holy) years actually began in the Middle Ages, when Pope Boniface VIII (1235–1303) proclaimed the first "holy year" in 1300 CE. Originally, he intended that such a year be held only once a century. But one of his successors, Pope Clement VI (1291–1352), who was one of the Avignon popes, proclaimed another jubilee year in 1350, only fifty years later, and declared that this should be their frequency.

From a Christian perspective, the purpose of these yearlong jubilees or holy years was to promote penance and conversion among the faithful. Some skeptics would add it was also intended to promote tourism, a not-so-infrequent by-product of holy years! The year especially involved making pilgrimages, whether to the Holy Land, to experience the land where Jesus lived and died and rose from the dead, or to Rome, to unite oneself more closely to the universal Church. Sometimes, pilgrimages to special shrines, particularly those associated with the Virgin Mary, were also encouraged. Closely tied to jubilee years is the controversial practice of granting indulgences for faithful participation in certain activities and religious rituals throughout the year.[1] Like the jubilee year of the Old Testament, holy years provide a chance to start again with "a clean slate." The main purpose of a Christian holy year, however, is clearly to transform one's life more and more in conformity to the gospel of Jesus Christ. It is to be an occasion for repentance and conversion, both individual and communal.

More recently, jubilee years have become occasions to celebrate specific themes or to promote devotions, such as to the Eucharist, the preeminent sacrament of the Church. Pope Benedict XVI, for instance, proclaimed the Year of Paul (June 28, 2008 to June 29, 2009) to commemorate the supposed bimillennium of the birth of the Apostle whose letters have so impacted Christianity.[2] He also proclaimed the "Year for Priests" (2009–10), intended, in part, to bolster the tarnished image of the Roman Catholic priesthood in the wake of the sexual abuse scandals that touched many countries. And finally, he promulgated the "Year of Faith" (October 11, 2012 to November 24, 2013), a more nebulous theme that was intended to tie into the Church's efforts of the "new evangelization."[3] Admittedly, in addition to drawing attention to specific themes or dimensions of the Christian faith, these holy years have generated a "cottage industry" of publications (of which, admittedly, this is one!) and promote pilgrimages, especially to Rome.

As mentioned in the acknowledgments, this book grew out of a series of articles for the Year of Mercy. Several assumptions are inherent in my approach. First, the book is based upon the assumption that the Bible's teaching remains perennially relevant to all the Christian faithful. It also has important messages for those in the modern world who may not be particularly familiar with its contents. Some people are fond of quoting the Bible to justify one or another position. Many times, they selectively cite the Bible, seeking only those texts that support their position. At other times, the cited texts are ripped entirely from their context, damaging the wholeness of the message. This book attempts to present the Bible's teaching on mercy in its proper context, encompassing both the Old and New Testaments, within the living Tradition of the Church. While it is not an exegetical work, as such, we will try to interpret the biblical texts in their proper contexts, without exploring too many technical details. Doing so will help ensure that the biblical message of mercy is not simply *our* reading but an authentic representation of the Bible's teaching.

A second assumption is that the teaching of Pope Francis on mercy remains relevant. It was central to the Year of Mercy and, to my mind, remains pertinent today. Since mercy is an obviously overarching theme of his papacy, the book incorporates some citations from his teachings, as well as other Church documents that broach the topic. While the book remains principally devoted to the biblical teaching on mercy, ecclesial insights will be evident from time to time, especially since they themselves are firmly rooted in the Bible's teaching.

A third assumption underlying this book is that we live in a world sorely in need of the message of mercy. Mercy is not merely a theme for a certain period. It is a more comprehensive and fundamental teaching, one that has largely been neglected in theological discourse. It should provide a basic orientation, at least for Christians, in a world where an alternative message of egoism, power, self-protection, populism, nationalism, terrorism, intolerance, and bullying is rampant. In a world filled with poverty, injustice, violence, hatred, and misery, mercy is a quality we need in full measure. This, at least, is my perspective and one that is honestly rooted in an authentic interpretation of the Bible.

Admittedly, exploring this project brought some trepidation. Many scholars talk about living in a postmodern, post-Christian world in which the Bible and Christian faith are considered irrelevant. Moreover, some speak of a "post-truth" society, one in which "alternative facts" and "fake news" win the day. It is a world where the message of power has seemingly swayed many people to look inward and search for self-protection. They yearn for a more rigid and controlled environment, where there is little left to chance, where lines are clearly drawn, where everything is black and white with no gray areas to cause confusion. In such a world, what role could mercy possibly play? Is mercy not merely a sign of weakness? A quality for "losers"? A leftover from a bygone era?

In such a world, mercy is even more urgently needed. Consequently, I have attempted to explain simply and clearly the biblical teaching on mercy, which I find eminently relevant and which, in fact, undergirds Pope Francis's dramatic call for a more merciful and compassionate Church in the modern world.

ABBREVIATIONS

AL	*Amoris Laetitia* (The Joy of Love), Post-synodal Apostolic Exhortation of Pope Francis (March 19, 2016)
BCE	Before the Common Era (= BC)
CCC	*Catechism of the Catholic Church*, 2nd ed. (1998)
CE	Common Era (= AD)
DM	*Dives in Misericordia* (Rich in Mercy), Encyclical Letter of Pope John Paul II (November 30, 1980)
EG	*Evangelii Gaudium* (The Joy of the Gospel), Encyclical Letter of Pope Francis (November 24, 2013), closing the Year of Faith
Gk.	Greek
GS	*Gaudium et Spes* (Joy and Hope), Vatican Council II's Pastoral Constitution on the Church in the Modern World (1965)
Heb.	Hebrew
LXX	The Septuagint (Greek translation of the Old Testament)
MM	*Misericordia et Misera* (Mercy and Misery), Apostolic Letter of Pope Francis (November 20, 2016), closing the Year of Mercy
MT	Masoretic Text (Hebrew Bible)

MV	*Misericordiae Vultus* (The Face of Mercy), Bull of Indiction of Pope Francis (April 11, 2015), proclaiming the Year of Mercy
NABRE	New American Bible, Revised Edition (2011)
NCR	*National Catholic Reporter*
NRSV	New Revised Standard Version of the Bible (1989)

CHAPTER 1

THE LANGUAGE OF MERCY

The LORD is merciful and gracious, / slow to anger and abounding in steadfast love. / He will not always accuse, nor will he keep his anger forever. / He does not deal with us according to our sins, / nor repay us according to our iniquities. / For as the heavens are high above the earth, / so great is his steadfast love toward those who fear him; / as far as the east is from the west, / so far he removes our transgressions from us. (Ps 103:8–12)

To begin our exploration of the theme of mercy, we need to understand the biblical vocabulary of mercy. We should remember that the Bible was composed mostly in Hebrew and Greek, with later copies being made in Latin. One cannot simply assume, then, that the biblical language of mercy is identical to that expressed in English. So let's begin with some linguistic research.

IN SEARCH OF A DEFINITION

My preparation for this project began with scholarly tools with which I was familiar. I began an initial search in a major biblical resource, the prestigious, multivolume *Anchor Bible Dictionary*.[1] Under the word *mercy* I found the entry "See *love*." Love is such a broad, all-encompassing, and even overworked topic that I was stymied for a moment. Did I really want to go down that road?

So I fled to an English dictionary[2] on my shelf and found the following main definitions for *mercy*: (1) "compassion or forbearance shown especially to an offender or to one subject to one's power"; (2) "a blessing that is an act of divine favor or compassion"; (3) "compassionate treatment of those in distress." Suggested synonyms were: *charity*, *clemency*, *grace*, and *leniency*. I did not see *love*.

What was going on here? Is the common English understanding of mercy different from what the Bible teaches? How are mercy and love interrelated? At the outset, we need to look closer at the background of mercy in the Bible, as well as glance at Pope Francis's own approach to the theme.

THE RICHNESS OF THE BIBLICAL VOCABULARY

Beginning with the Old Testament, we find several words that express the concept of mercy. The challenge, of course, is to find appropriate translation equivalents, not always an easy task when words have a wide range of meaning.

PRINCIPAL BIBLICAL VOCABULARY OF MERCY

OLD TESTAMENT			
HEBREW TERM	**LXX TRANSLATION**	**BASIC MEANING**	**OBSERVATIONS**
ḥesed (*chesed*)	*eleeō* (v.) *eleos* (n.)	"steadfast faithfulness" or "kindness" or "mercy"; used in the context of a covenant relationship	used ca. 245x in the MT; usually in singular form
rḥm (*racham*) (occurs in verbal, nominal, and adjectival forms)	*oiktirō* (v.) *eleeō* (v.) *eleos* (n.)	"compassion" or "mercy"	verb used ca. 49x in MT; connotes deep emotion; possibly related to *reḥem* (womb)
ḥnn (*chanan*) (v.) *ḥēn* (n.) *ḥannûn* (adj.)	*oiktirō* *charis* *oiktirmōn*/ *eleēmōn*	"be gracious" or "show favor"; always used of God "grace" or "favor" (always singular) "gracious"	basic divine attribute noun occurs ca. 67x in MT adj. occurs with *raḥûm* (adj.), "merciful"

NEW TESTAMENT		
GREEK TERM	**BASIC MEANING**	**OBSERVATIONS**
eleeō, *eleaō* (v.) *eleos* (n.) *eleēmosynē* (n.)	"have mercy"; "have pity"; "exercise mercy" "mercy"; "compassion"; "pity" "kindness"; "pity"; "alms"	verb *eleeō* used in 29 NT passages, the noun in 27; neither is used in John and Acts; *eleaō* used only 3 times in NT in the NT usually restricted to almsgiving, thus mercy or kindness to the poor

Continued

Principal Biblical Vocabulary of Mercy *continued*

GREEK TERM	BASIC MEANING	OBSERVATIONS
oiktirō (v.) *oiktirmos* (n.) *oiktirmōn* (adj.)	"have compassion" "heartfelt compassion or mercy" "compassionate"; "merciful"	expresses sympathy and pity; in the NT, is very similar to the use of the root *elee-*
splanchnizomai (v.) *splanchnōn* (n.)	"have pity"; "have compassion" lit. "inner organs"; occurs always in plural; refers to the physical inner organs but figuratively is used of deep emotions	in the Synoptic Gospels used of Jesus' deep compassion for people

One Hebrew root for mercy is *rḥm* (*rakham*), which has verbal, nominal, and adjectival forms. It is related to the same root that means "womb" or "belly," which likely shows its connection to deep human emotions. It also implies a "feminine" dimension in its connection to the womb. The verb is used in Isaiah, for example, in the powerful claim of the Prophet that God remains faithful:

> Can a mother forget her nursing child, or show no compassion (Heb. *mērachēm*) for the child of her womb? Even should these forget, yet I will not forget you. (Isa 49:15, au. trans.)

From its multiple occurrences, the root *rḥm* clearly expresses compassion, affection, tenderness, and even pity. One should also note that this Hebrew word is rarely used as an attribute of human beings (e.g., Ps 112:4), although it is anthropomorphic language (i.e., resembling human nature). It is used almost exclusively of God. It is found in some key biblical expressions like Exodus 34:6–7, which proclaims that God (the LORD) is "a God *merciful* and gracious, / slow to anger, / and abounding in steadfast love and faithfulness, / keeping steadfast love for the thousandth generation, / forgiving iniquity and transgression and sin" (italics mine, see also Deut 4:31). What we should not miss in this passage is the line immediately following: "…yet by no means clearing the guilty, / but visiting the iniquity of the parents / upon the children / and the children's children, / to the third and the fourth generation" (Exod 34:7). In this context, mercy and graciousness are not a free pass to sin and expect forgiveness with no consequences; God is *both* merciful and just. Mercy is forgiving *and* demanding.

Another Hebrew word for mercy, often paired with *rḥm* (as in Exod 34:6), is the root *ḥnn* (*chanan*) whose basic meaning is "grace" or "favor." Thus, the prophet Joel calls the people to repentance because God is by nature "*gracious* and merciful" (Joel 2:13), even though God's favorable disposition is also oriented to those who are righteous (e.g., Ps 84:12[11]). The verbal form normally means "to show favor" or "to be gracious."

A third Hebrew word, and by far the most frequently used, is *ḥesed*, which the NRSV usually translates as "steadfast love" but never with the word *mercy*. Most English Bibles, though, translate this word with "mercy." The late biblical scholar John L. McKenzie, who single-handedly compiled one of the most impressive Bible dictionaries of the twentieth century, calls this choice of translation "unfortunate" because the word has multiple meanings, depending on the context.[3] *Ḥesed* is, in fact, a key biblical concept of God's steadfast love, faithfulness, loyalty, and kindness. It is closely tied to the notion of covenant (Heb. *berith*). God shows his loyalty in remaining faithful to the covenant freely extended to his chosen people (e.g., Pss 89:28; 106:45; 107:1–2, 19–21; Isa 54:10; 55:3; cf. Pss 25:10; 86:13–15; Dan 9:4). The notion certainly includes mercy, since God's attitude toward Israel, the chosen covenant people, is one that tolerates innumerable violations of the covenant. Yet it shows God's constancy in this less-than-ideal situation. While the word's etymology is unknown, it occurs some 245 times in the Old Testament, in both narrative and poetic contexts. Interestingly, in many biblical contexts this word implies that the one who receives this "steadfast love" is also expected to reciprocate with the same quality (e.g., Gen 21:23, 27; Josh 12:2, 14). Thus, a quality of God is expected to become a virtue among human beings, even in their dealings with one another.

The Septuagint (the Greek translation of the Old Testament symbolized by LXX) translates *ḥesed* most frequently with the Greek noun *eleos* ("mercy"); the Latin Vulgate uses *misericordia*, the easily identifiable root of the French, Spanish, and Italian words for "mercy." In fact, the official hymn composed for the Year of Mercy contained a Latin refrain: *Misericordes sicut Pater* ("Merciful like the Father"), which was also the motto for the year. The verbal form in Greek, "to show mercy" or "to be merciful," is normally the related verb *eleeō* ("have mercy"). The Septuagint links this vocabulary of *mercy*, then, to *ḥesed*, thus intimately tying steadfast love to mercy.

The New Testament, likewise, uses the same Greek terms to express the concept of mercy, whether in relationship to Jesus' public ministry or in explaining God's attitude toward human beings. For example, in Matthew's Gospel, Jesus cites an Old Testament prophetic passage twice to correct the false orientation of his opponents toward legalism: "I desire *mercy* (Gk. *eleon*) not sacrifice" (Matt 9:13; 12:7; see also Hos 6:6). When people are near Jesus, they often beg for mercy: "Have *mercy* on me, Lord" (Matt 15:22; see also Matt 17:15; 20:30; etc.). This is the same expression used in the pre-Vatican II liturgy in Greek and preserved in Gregorian chant, *Kyrie, eleison*—"Lord, have mercy." It is a plea for mercy expressed by those most in need of it—sinners.

Paul's letters show special appreciation for the vocabulary of *mercy*, which we will examine more closely in chapter 5. Paul sees God's mercy at work in the mystery of how the Gentiles have been privileged to be welcomed among the chosen people. But God's mercy will somehow also be shown to the original chosen people,

Israel (Rom 11:25–32). For Paul, mercy is an aspect of God's activity in salvation history. It is closely related to God's "grace" (Gk. *charis*) and "peace" (Gk. *eirēnē*; Heb. *shalōm*; cf. Gal 6:16; 1 Tim 1:2), the two expressions he uses regularly as greetings at the beginning and end of his letters.

OVERVIEW

What can we conclude from this quick survey of the biblical vocabulary? There are four fundamental observations based on the overall biblical orientation toward mercy. First, mercy encompasses many interrelated qualities. It is closely associated with compassion, faithfulness, steadfastness, tenderness, grace, favor, forgiveness, pity, and so on, including love. Because of this diversity, it is dangerous to reduce the concept to one word, such as *mercy*. Rather, it is a rich concept, as dictionaries indicate. Yet, one can explore the nuances of the idea in various passages of the Bible, for context can provide nuanced interpretations otherwise missed.

Second, the Bible teaches that mercy is most evidently a quality or attribute of God toward human beings, especially toward the covenant people whom he has invited into relationship. In this covenant context, mercy has many dimensions. It is faithfulness, steadfastness, loving-kindness, graciousness, and showing favor to human beings. It also implies infinite patience. The God of the covenant is both merciful and patient with his wayward people.

A third aspect is the reciprocal dimension of mercy in the Bible. Those who receive mercy from God are called to emulate it. This is not a minor point. Mercy is not simply something one receives, although God bestows it freely, and with no strings attached. Receiving it, however, brings with it a responsibility to share it with others. Like any gift, it is even better when shared. Once received, we are to pass it on. Mercy is thus not only a divine quality or attribute but also a human virtue. It is something to be fostered in the arena of human interaction.

Finally, although mercy is a gift freely given by God and not something earned or deserved, it is not simply a free pass to do whatever we want and then expect that God will gloss over our failings or sinfulness. Once more, in the context of a covenant relationship, God extends mercy time and again, expecting that there is human resolve to rectify that which is lacking in human faithfulness to God's covenant. Mercy is thus related to God's justice as well. God is both merciful and just, kind and demanding, forgiving and capable of judging. This complex concept warrants separate investigation on its own, and will be addressed in the following chapters.

These are brief conclusions, and more could be said. But the essential understanding is well founded. The Bible's teaching on mercy is broad and more complex than we perhaps initially perceive. The point of the next five chapters is to flesh out this concept in greater detail by examining various writings in the Bible and gleaning from them more information about the mercy of God. A concluding chapter will pull the threads of the biblical instruction together and address how such a teaching might be important in today's world. Before proceeding, however, we should glance briefly at a more contemporary context of the theme of mercy, especially as seen in Pope Francis, whose teaching is based upon the biblical notion.

THE YEAR OF MERCY

Although the Year of Mercy is now long past, we can review some of its impact as seen in the papacy of Pope Francis. Most evident is that mercy is the primary theme of his papacy. His episcopal motto, taken from Bede the Venerable's commentary on the Gospel of Matthew, is the Latin expression *miserando atque eligendo*, which means "by having mercy and by choosing." It refers to the mercy with which Jesus chose Matthew as an apostle (Matt 9:9).

The Language of Mercy

From the opening days of his pontificate, Pope Francis has consistently spoken of mercy and called for a more merciful Church. Here, it is sufficient to point out just some elements of this orientation that have been expressed well by the pope's apparently preferred theologian Cardinal Walter Kasper. Just prior to Pope Francis's election as supreme pontiff on March 13, 2013, Kasper had published a book on the theme of mercy titled *Mercy: The Essence of the Gospel and the Key to Christian Life*.[4] During his first Sunday Angelus discourse at St. Peter's Square on March 17, 2013, the pope himself drew attention to the impact of this book on his own thought. The pope's own words are worth quoting:

> In the past few days, I have been reading a book by a Cardinal—Cardinal Kasper, a clever theologian, a good theologian—on mercy. And that book did me a lot of good, but do not think I am promoting my cardinals' books! Not at all! Yet it has done me so much good, so much good....Cardinal Kasper said that feeling mercy, that this word changes everything. This is the best thing we can feel: it changes the world. A little mercy makes the world less cold and more just. We need to understand properly this mercy of God, this merciful Father who is so patient....Let us remember the Prophet Isaiah who says that even if our sins were scarlet, God's love would make them white as snow. This mercy is beautiful![5]

Although Cardinal Kasper must have been pleased with the promotion, more important was the book's unforeseen impact on the direction of Francis's papacy.

Subsequently, Kasper published another book that addressed this very issue. Titled *Pope Francis' Revolution of Tenderness and Love: Theological and Pastoral Perspectives*,[6] the book lays out the multiple aspects of the Holy Father's desire to shape a Church that is more tender, more open, more loving, more forgiving—in short, more merciful. Kasper even labels it a "revolution of mercy." From these brief examples, it is easy to see how deeply the theme of mercy permeates Pope Francis's vision. In addition, there are substantive biblical and theological underpinnings for it, which the present book will endeavor to explain.

Symbolically, the fact that Pope Francis chose to issue the official papal bull proclaiming the extraordinary Holy Year of Mercy at First Vespers on Divine Mercy Sunday, the Second Sunday of Easter 2015, reinforced his desire to place mercy at the very center of the contemporary Church's life. This act reminds us, too, that it was Pope John Paul II who designated that Sunday as Divine Mercy Sunday, based upon his personal devotion to the teachings of Saint Faustina Kowalska on the importance of divine mercy. That the notion of mercy has struck a chord among many Catholics is seen in the popularity of the devotions tied to Divine Mercy Sunday. It is beyond the scope of this book to examine this devotion, but before expanding our study of other sections of the Bible's teaching on mercy, we will quickly look at the papal perspective on this theme that emerges from one of Pope Francis's key writings, The Joy of the Gospel (*Evangelii Gaudium*).

EVANGELII GAUDIUM

The post-synodal apostolic exhortation, *Evangelii Gaudium* (2013) grew out of the synod on the new evangelization (October 2012). The text uses the word *mercy* (in the English text) thirty-two times. Although the pope's exposé is rich, we can summarize his main approach with three principal concepts.

The first one is the concrete nature of mercy. Pope Francis emphasizes that mercy is not simply an interior attitude, or, dare I say, a pious platitude. It is very concrete. It involves what the Church has traditionally called "the corporal works of mercy," which the

Catechism of the Catholic Church describes in detail (CCC §2447). The classic list of these works of mercy are the following:

- feeding the hungry;
- giving water to the thirsty;
- clothing the naked;
- sheltering the homeless;
- visiting the sick and imprisoned;
- ransoming captives; and
- burying the dead.

They are inspired by the famous passage from Matthew's Gospel, the parable of the sheep and goats (Matt 25:31–46), which describes judgment day. When the righteous (sheep) are rewarded with admission to the kingdom of heaven, the rationale the divine Judge (Christ, the Son of Man) gives is simply this:

> For I was hungry and you gave me food, I was thirsty and you gave me something to drink, I was a stranger and you welcomed me, I was naked and you gave me clothing, I was sick and you took care of me, I was in prison and you visited me. (Matt 25:35–36)

The "I" in this passage is Christ, but the actions are directed to the needy around us. The Matthean text clearly means that what we do to the "least" of our brothers and sisters, is what we do—or do not do—to Christ himself. Thus, the "goats"—the unrighteous who ignored the sufferings of their neighbor—are sent off to eternal punishment for not having attended to these obligations.

Later Christian tradition, using passages from the Bible, identified a comparable list of "spiritual works of mercy," which include:

- to instruct the ignorant;
- to counsel the doubtful;

- to admonish sinners;
- to bear patiently those who wrong us;
- to forgive offenses;
- to console the afflicted; and
- to pray for the living and the dead.

Together, the corporal and spiritual works of mercy constitute a concrete Christian program for mercy.

During his pontificate, Pope Francis has explicitly called for the Church to become concretely more merciful:

> The Church must be a place of mercy freely given, where everyone can feel welcomed, loved, forgiven and encouraged to live the good life of the Gospel. (*EG* 114)

Mercy makes people feel welcomed, loved, and forgiven. But we should note well that this teaching is hardly new. The *Catechism* teaches that the Church promotes the mercy of God among human beings, especially through the sacrament of reconciliation (§2040). The Church, by its nature, is supposed to be an instrument of God's reconciling mercy.

Closely tied to this point is a second, namely, the orientation of mercy toward "those most in need" (*EG* 194, 252). For Pope Francis, this means primarily the poor, the displaced, the immigrants, the marginalized, the persecuted (for race, religion, ethnicity, or sexual orientation), and the powerless. He looks at the modern world and perceives an enormous, and growing, gulf between the "haves" and "have nots." He sees the vast numbers of dispossessed in comparison to the much smaller number of rich and successful. He sees refugees who are rejected and despised. He sees people turning in on themselves and not reaching out to others, especially the poor. Thus, he calls for "mercy" toward these masses. It involves tenderness and pity, an outreach that touches those who are most in need of even the basics of human survival.

A third aspect also comes to the fore. Invoking the biblical teaching, Francis recalls forcefully that mercy is ultimately a divine action. We are ourselves, first, recipients of God's mercy. It is in God's very nature to be merciful, most readily seen in the gift of his own Son to the world for the sake of our salvation (*EG* 285). Pope Francis also cites a passage from the great theologian Saint Thomas Aquinas (1225–74) that asserts the priority of mercy over all the other virtues, making it tantamount to love. Thomas writes,

> In itself mercy is the greatest of the virtues, since all the others revolve around it and, more than this, it makes up for their deficiencies. This is particular to the superior virtue, and as such it is proper to God to have mercy, through which his omnipotence is manifested to the greatest degree. (*EG* 37)

We can add that the *Catechism* calls mercy one of the principal "fruits" of charity (§1829), thus tying it closely to love in action.

PRIESTS–AGENTS OF GOD'S MERCY

One of Pope Francis's actions during the Year of Mercy was to issue a special call to priests to be more effectively agents of mercy. He did this in several ways. One was that he extended the ability to hear confessions to members of the St. Pius X Society, the ultraconservative breakaways from the Catholic Church who argue for a return to pre–Vatican II perspectives, especially in liturgy. This was a remarkable action, and it showed how deeply the pope felt about extending the outreach of mercy through the sacrament of reconciliation.

A related gesture was the "initiative of *24 Hours for the Lord,* to be celebrated on the Friday and Saturday preceding the Fourth Week of Lent" (*MV* 17). It was to be an occasion in dioceses throughout the world to offer the sacrament of reconciliation continuously, calling on priests to become "authentic signs of the Father's mercy." There can be no doubt that behind the pope's vision is the frank acknowledgment that one unpleasant experience in the confessional can damage a person's confidence in the sacrament for a long time. He thus urged priests to become more effective, more compassionate confessors.

Another remarkable gesture was the pope's designation of numerous priests to become "missionaries of mercy" during the Year of Mercy. He desired to grant them the authority to pardon even those sins reserved to the Holy See, so that the breadth of their mandate as confessors will be even clearer.

> They will be, above all, living signs of the Father's readiness to welcome those in search of his pardon. They will be missionaries of mercy because they will be facilitators of a truly human encounter, a source of liberation, rich with responsibility for overcoming obstacles and taking up the new life of Baptism again. (*MV* 18)

Interestingly, the pope later (November 21, 2016) extended indefinitely this special permission for priests in exercising the sacrament of reconciliation in relation to offering forgiveness for the sin of abortion, which was normally reserved to bishops to forgive.

Finally, the pope himself led a three-part retreat for more than six thousand priests from around the world. He gave them three distinct conferences in three locations in Rome: the Basilica of St. John Lateran Basilica, which is the pope's own cathedral; the Basilica of St. Mary Major; and the Basilica of St. Paul Outside-the-Walls. The conferences were profound reflections on mercy in the ministry of priests. Among his many nuggets of wisdom were the following, which are good examples of Francis's penchant for pastoral preaching:

- "By now you have realized that in Spanish I like to use "mercy" as a verb: "We have to 'show mercy' [*misericordiar*] in order to 'receive mercy' [*ser misericordiados*]."
- "We cannot meditate on mercy without it turning into action."
- "The one who shows mercy and the one to whom mercy is shown become equals."
- "God keeps forgiving, even though he sees how hard it is for his grace to take root in the parched and rocky soil of our hearts."
- "Today we can think of the Church as a 'field hospital.'...There is need to cure the wounds, so many wounds! So many wounds!"

He also invoked figures such as Saint Francis of Assisi and the Virgin Mary to call priests to engage more forcefully in the ministry of mercy. He labeled Psalm 50(51)—King David's eloquent plea for mercy that is enshrined in the Liturgy of the Hours every Friday at morning prayer—the "Magnificat of mercy." It expresses perfectly the humble attitude that a priest must have as a minister of mercy, conscious of his own need for mercy. Recall the first words of this Psalm:

> Have mercy on me, O God,
>   according to your steadfast love;
> according to your abundant mercy
>   blot out my transgressions.
> Wash me thoroughly from my iniquity,
>   and cleanse me from my sin.
>
> (Ps 51:1–2)

With such images, the pope preached a retreat that, according to those who attended the sessions, evoked deep emotions. One can still hear references to these reflections when priests recall, "Mercy is a verb" and "The Church is a field hospital!"

DISQUIETING REACTIONS

Frankly, this talk of mercy, and especially Pope Francis's evident desire to make the Church's practice concretely more merciful—for example, discussions about finding ways to address the genuine problem of divorce and remarriage in the Church—have made many people nervous, with even some members of the hierarchy expressing alarm. One need only think of the extended controversy that surrounded the two special synods of bishops on marriage and divorce (2014 and 2015) that ultimately led to Pope Francis's post-synodal apostolic exhortation *Amoris Laetitia* ("The Joy of Love") in 2016. Some accused the pope of having promoted confusion and division by his teaching that seemingly opened the door to allowing divorced and remarried Catholics to receive communion, a practice deemed threatening to the absolute sanctity of the sacrament of marriage. Others defended the pope, pointing out that the exhortation simply calls for a more pastoral treatment of divorced and remarried people in the Church. It was not, they say, a watering down of the doctrine or theology of marriage and its absolute indissolubility. Rather, it was an attempt to encourage a pastoral approach to those who find themselves in extremely difficult marital situations, sometimes through no fault of their own. The exhortation (especially the controversial chapter 8) seems to promote the preference for the priority of individual conscience over strict interpretation of Church law. For some, this is too loose an approach. It opens the door to laxity and, indeed, would allegedly overturn Jesus' prohibition of divorce and remarriage (see Matt 19:9) and the Church's longstanding practice of the same prohibition.

Our point here is not to enter the intricacies of a doctrinal and moral debate on marriage and divorce. This is not a book on moral theology; nor is it a critique of the papal apostolic exhortation. Rather, the focus is on the question of how mercy impacts the day-to-day ministry of the Church. Nevertheless, this controversy honestly raised many questions about mercy and how it is to be applied in the Church. Does becoming more merciful mean that one becomes "soft" on sin? Does mercy promote laxity? Does it mean one tolerates violations of Church law or magisterial teaching? Does it compromise the faith? Does it reward bad behavior?

These are the kinds of questions that some pose when they hear talk of mercy. Some are worried that it will lead to a watered-down Catholicism, or promote a lax mentality. Yet, a careful reading of Pope Francis's messages on mercy hardly seems to warrant such fears. He has not proposed changing any doctrines. Moreover, he has explicitly upheld Church teaching on such hot-button items as abortion, traditional family structure, and restricting priestly ordination to men. Nonetheless, his call for a more merciful, forgiving, and loving Church surely touches many aspects of the Bible's wide-ranging teaching on mercy. Jesus himself was attacked for promoting mercy and forgiveness in the face of those who thought it their duty to defend the religious requirements of the day by condemning those who seemingly bent the rules. Just a few examples will illustrate this fact.

In Matthew, for instance, some Pharisees ask Jesus' disciples why he eats with tax collectors and sinners (9:11).[7] Their implication is clear. They consider it improper to socialize with those who are considered unworthy. Jesus' response, referring to the divine call for mercy emphasized by the prophet Hosea, is to affirm that he came to call sinners, not the righteous (9:12–13; see also Hos 6:6). Another example concerns the situation of the man with the withered hand that Jesus encounters on the Sabbath (Matt 12:9–14). Again, some Pharisees challenge Jesus with the question of whether it is lawful to heal on the Sabbath. Jesus uses the example of someone whose sheep falls into a pit on the Sabbath, noting that that person would not hesitate to fetch it out. Then he says, "How much more valuable is a human being than a sheep! So it is lawful to do good on the sabbath" (v. 12), and proceeds to heal the man's hand. Or yet another example that occurs during a long denunciation of the tendency of the Jewish leaders to demand onerous burdens upon people while neglecting the "weightier matters of the law: justice and mercy and faith" (23:23). These are what count. Jesus' message is clear: even the rules sometimes must be bent to enact the more important matters God demands: mercy and justice. In this teaching of Jesus, one hears an echo of the Old Testament prophet Micah, who taught,

> He [God] has told you, O mortal, what is good;
>   and what does the LORD require of you
> but to do justice, and to love kindness,
>   and to walk humbly with your God?
>
> (Mic 6:8)

With the special Year of Mercy, the Church had an opportunity to reflect in more depth on the biblical and magisterial teaching about this broad and complex topic. The task now becomes how to make mercy an ongoing living reality, whose impact can truly shape a better world. Given developments around the world at the end of the Year of Mercy, it was evident that there still remain many obstacles to implementing Pope Francis's pastoral vision of mercy. He issued the invitation; our part is to continue to respond. The biblical analysis offered in the following chapters will provide the proper foundation for advancing the topic further as we wrestle with the challenge of becoming more merciful, like the Father.

REFLECTION QUESTIONS

1. How widespread is the language of "mercy" in the Bible? Do you consider mercy to be a primary theme

in the Bible? If so, what is particularly attractive about the theme? Do you see any limitations to it?

2. What is the relationship between mercy and love? Are they the same thing? If not, how do they differ?
3. How would you relate mercy to forgiveness? Does mercy require forgiveness? Do you think God can be both merciful and just at the same time? Why or why not?
4. What comes to mind when the Bible speaks of God's "steadfast love"? Can you give any examples from the Bible of this dimension of God's character?
5. Why did Pope Francis proclaim an extraordinary jubilee Year of Mercy? Do you think it had a positive effect? From your own experience, what remains to be done to truly implement the vision imparted by this extraordinary holy year?

CHAPTER 2

IS GOD *REALLY* MERCIFUL?

AN OLD TESTAMENT PERSPECTIVE

> *The LORD passed before him, and proclaimed, / "The LORD, the LORD, / a God merciful and gracious, / slow to anger, / and abounding in steadfast love and faithfulness."* (Exod 34:6)

Having dealt with basic biblical vocabulary of mercy, we now explore in greater depth an Old Testament perspective on mercy.

With the Old Testament, we face an immediate challenge. Many have preconceived notions about the Old Testament. They are troubled by passages that seemingly reflect anything but a merciful attitude. In fact, many Christians think of the God of the Old Testament as a God of justice and vengeance, with precious little interest in mercy.[1] If mercy is so important in the Christian tradition, then why does the Bible seem so filled with violence and vengeance? Here it is helpful to recall that this is not a new viewpoint. Already in the early Church, a heretic named Marcion (ca. 85–160) forcefully promoted the idea that the image of God found in the

Old Testament contradicted the message of love and mercy found in the New Testament, especially in the portrait of Jesus in Luke's Gospel, and rejected outright the Old Testament. The Church strongly condemned this view and insisted on retaining the Old Testament as the authentic "Word of God," along with the New Testament. This remains the Church's teaching today. This fact, however, does not address the question of how mercy fits into the overall message of the Old Testament.

THE "BIG PICTURE"

Let's first examine what we might call the "big picture" presented in the Old Testament. Viewed from a position of faith, as all Christians read the Bible, the Old Testament offers a unified and cyclic story of creation, sin, redemption, and re-creation. It is a story filled with peaks and valleys, with tales of violence and destruction, but also narratives of forgiveness and new beginnings.

God's very first act, recounted in the Book of Genesis, is a generous act of love. Out of chaos and void, God creates the universe. God brings order and beauty into creation and gives authority over it to human beings (Gen 1:1—2:3). Quickly, however, Adam and Eve—the "first" humans, representatives of all humanity—succumb to temptation (personified by a talking serpent!) and seek to become like God. Their act of eating from the forbidden tree of the knowledge of good and evil is idolatry. It is an attempt to make themselves "gods" rather than remain as creatures, God's handiwork, and the pinnacle of God's creative activity. They were made in God's image, male and female, yet they attempted to supplant God (1:26–27). In such a brief time, the creation that God had judged "very good" went awry. This is not God's fault, but humanity's weakness. Quickly, human violence comes to the fore when Cain kills his brother Abel (4:1–16). Interestingly, God's just punishment for this murderous act, committed out of jealousy, is not the death penalty, but banishment from the land, forced to wander the earth.

The point of this quick overview is that it sets a pattern. The rest of the Old Testament might be said to be the consistent repetition of God extending to Israel (and humanity) the hand of friendship—seen in covenant after covenant—and human sinfulness in rejecting that offer. One sees the pattern in the stories of Noah, Abraham and the patriarchs, Moses and the giving of the Torah (law), Israel in Egypt, and so on. God's seemingly inexhaustible patience with the chosen people, Israel, always leaves room for one more chance. It is the story of covenantal fidelity on God's part. It is a tale of friendship offered in a covenant relationship, violation of that covenant, just punishment for human sinfulness, and a merciful offer to begin again.

This scenario is, of course, an oversimplification. Yet the pattern is real. God's final word is mercy. So important was it to the scribes who preserved the Hebrew Bible (Old Testament) to conclude it on a hopeful note that the last book, Malachi, concludes with a promise for the future. In the context of once more calling for the observance of God's law, the Torah given to Moses on Mount Sinai (Horeb), Malachi says,

> Lo, I will send you the prophet Elijah before the great and terrible day of the LORD comes. He will turn the hearts of parents to their children and the hearts of children to their parents, so that I will not come and strike the land with a curse. (4:5–6)

While there is the ominous reference to possible destruction, two images sound a positive note. The first concerns the return of the prophet Elijah, the precursor of the coming "terrible" day of judgment. We should notice, here, that the word *terrible* does not mean "disastrous" but "fearful," "awesome," or "to be reverenced." The second is the comforting image that parents and children will be reconciled. Human disagreements would not predominate. God's patience would not finally run out. Christians immediately saw in this prophecy the image of John the Baptist, precursor to Jesus Christ, the embodiment of mercy. Matthew's Gospel, in fact, makes the connection between Elijah and John the Baptist explicit (11:12–14).

The big picture, then, is that while the human tendency toward sin remains, God's steadfast love and mercy are even more reliable. When we descend into the valleys of self-indulgence, violence, and evil deeds, God offers to raise us up on the heights, to the dignity for which we were made in God's image.

NARROWING THE FOCUS

The big picture may offer some comfort, but there are still troubling passages in the Old Testament that raise questions. We will examine just a few here.[2]

One of the most famous passages concerns the norm of "eye for eye, tooth for tooth" (Exod 21:24). In our day, those who favor the death penalty are fond of quoting this passage. (Curiously, they do not quote Jesus' apparent abrogation of this principle [Matt 5:38–39].) Yet the context of the passage is important. In Old Testament times, vengeance often took the form of unlimited retaliation. In Exodus, the principle attempts to delimit retaliation to a reasonable, proportional level. It took centuries to grow beyond even this limited form of vengeance, but it does not provide blanket approval for revenge, even less so considering Jesus' teaching.

Other troubling passages concern the multiple stories in which God asks Israel to annihilate or exterminate their enemies (see Deut 20:17). Apart from the question of whether such accounts are rooted in history, these passages are disquieting because they raise questions of whether God does indeed promote a vengeful attitude. Two comments help to put such passages in perspective.

First, the point of total extermination of one's enemy in the Old Testament was, in part, to prevent Israel from using warfare for personal gain. To offer up everything and everyone of the enemy to God was a way of dampening the desire for the spoils of war, either goods or slaves. Warfare was legitimate for defense, but it was not to be a means of profit.

Second, the primary context of such passages is in God's protection of his chosen people, Israel, in the face of nations that practiced truly abhorrent rituals, like child sacrifice (Deut 12:31; 18:10–12). God puts the chosen people first but also demands of them ethical uprightness in contrast to some of the pagan practices of their enemies. Israel was to be a sign of the "otherness" of their God. Their way was to be more demanding. They were to take the ethical "high road" and call other nations ultimately to follow in their footsteps toward the one God of all creation. Such extreme acts, then, were to reinforce Israel's call to a higher moral standard in a context of extremely diverse ethical practices.

Another example comes from the prayers of Israel, especially the psalms. What does one make of the concluding wish in Psalm 137?

> Happy shall they be who take your little ones
> and dash them against the rock!
>
> (137:9)

The Church rightly has excised this line from the Liturgy of the Hours when this psalm is prayed, but why is it in the Old Testament at all? The context is again important. This psalm expresses the dire emotion of Israel during the traumatic exile in Babylon (ca. 597–539 BCE). The psalm is a lament that bemoans their terrible fate. Their enemies not only enslave but also mock them, asking them to sing one of their songs (Ps 137:3). In this situation, they cry out to God, wishing a most hideous suffering upon their tormentors. We can perhaps empathize with this emotion, but there is no evidence that it became a concrete reality. Indeed, when Israel finally returned from exile and could rebuild Jerusalem and their lives, it was a pagan ruler, Cyrus of Persia, who was God's instrument of their rebirth (Isa 44:28; 2 Chr 36:22–23). Moreover, the exile paradoxically afforded the Jews occasion to learn about other cultures, and it even led to some intermarriage. Such prayers of vengeance, then, sometimes reflect the intense emotion of the moment, but they do not thereby constitute a principle for all time.

A POSITIVE APPROACH

The previous section represents a somewhat negative approach to the question of mercy in the Old Testament. In other words, such passages that trouble many people do exist, but there are often explanations that can help us understand them better, or perhaps mitigate their impact. There is, however, a more compelling reason to see in the Old Testament a message of mercy. Despite the presence of numerous passages on violence or vengeance, there are also innumerable passages in which God's merciful, and even tender, side appears. We will begin with general observations and then analyze several sections of the Old Testament for specific teaching on mercy, all of which constitute a "positive" approach to the theme.

MERCY AS A CHARACTERISTIC OF GOD

The orientation to God's mercy in the Old Testament is rooted in the story of Creation, which we summarized earlier, and then the story of the exodus. Both imply something very basic in the understanding of God's nature as a merciful One. Both are tied to the mystery of divine election, which is nothing less than the mystery of love. (So there is a connection between mercy and love!)

The Creation story itself (Gen 1—2) is really a story of overflowing love. According to Genesis 1, God simply chooses to "create," to impose order on the chaos of the universe. It is God's intention to organize this world and to make of it a "garden" for the very pinnacle of creation, the human person, the one who is made in God's own image, both male and female (1:27). No reason is given for this gesture. Contrary to other creation myths among pagan peoples at the time, Genesis asserts that creation is purposeful, does not derive from evil forces, and that all creation is good. As God rests on the Sabbath and surveys all he has made, the text says, "God saw everything that he had made, and indeed, it was very good" (1:31). When evil enters the picture, it is not God's doing. It is the result of human folly (the sin of Adam and Eve recounted in Genesis 3).

While it is true that God punishes Adam and Eve by expelling them from the garden of Eden and forcing them to work for a living, it is also true that, as the mythological[3] stories of Genesis 3—11 continue, God gives multiple chances to human beings to start again. This is particularly true of the Noah story (Gen 6—9). Noah and his family, along with the animals on the ark, all survive the great flood, which was humanity's just punishment, the result of extreme human sinfulness. God then makes a new "covenant" with them. It is another chance to start again. The sign of this covenant is the rainbow (9:16), a heavenly sign that represents hope and a new beginning "after the storm." The point here is to note that God does not *permanently* punish the people. God freely grants a new occasion to set things right, to get off to a good start once more.

After the act of Creation, the most consequential evidence of God's merciful actions toward the chosen people is the exodus event. When God calls Moses from the burning bush to enlist his leadership in effecting the exodus event, the text explains God's motivation with the following words:

> Then the LORD said, "I have observed the misery of my people who are in Egypt; I have heard their cry on account of their taskmasters. Indeed, I know their sufferings, and I have come down to deliver them from

> the Egyptians, and to bring them up out of that land to a good and broad land, a land flowing with milk and honey." (Exod 3:7–8)

What we notice here is God's reaction to the misery of the Hebrews in Egypt. He sees their misery; he hears their cry; he knows their sufferings; and he comes to deliver them from their bondage. In short, God is entirely merciful on their behalf. As the story of the exodus is told in the Bible, the Israelites were slaves in Egypt and were suffering. Only when God raises up important leaders like the siblings Moses, Aaron, and Miriam, does God set the forces of liberation in motion. Mercy is God's "saving help"[4] that comes when it is most needed in the history of Israel.

This gracious action would lead to the covenant, the sacred agreement between God and Israel, which also involves the commitment on the part of God's people to observe the commandments (lit. the ten "words" [Heb. *devarim*]), in return for God's constant faithfulness (Exod 20). This agreement ultimately ties God's mercy ever after to faithfulness to this covenant, as expressed in the Book of Deuteronomy:

> Because the LORD your God is a merciful God, he will neither abandon you nor destroy you; he will not forget the covenant with your ancestors that he swore to them. (4:31)

Yet another aspect of the Old Testament perspective touches the rationale for God's mercy. A singular passage in the Book of Deuteronomy contains the only explanation offered for why God chose Israel to be the covenant people. I know of no more profound explanation in the Bible:

> It was not because you were more numerous than any other people that the LORD set his heart on you and

> chose you—for you were the fewest of all peoples. It was because the LORD loved you and kept the oath that he swore to your ancestors, that the LORD has brought you out with a mighty hand, and redeemed you from the house of slavery, from the hand of Pharaoh king of Egypt. (7:7–8)

Greatness had nothing to do with it; neither did size or significance. The only two motivations for God's kind actions toward "little" Israel are love and faithfulness to the covenantal oath rooted in the experience of the exodus. God's actions, then, are nothing less than mercy, steadfast fidelity, and love. God can be no other. It is his mercy that sets him apart from all other gods. Israel's God is consequently unique. Moreover, his merciful actions are nothing short of the mystery of divine election. It is a gift freely given that God has chosen to bestow on a people.

What this description affirms is that mercy is an essential characteristic of the God of Israel. It is not merely that Israel cries out for and expects mercy, but that God is also willing to extend it liberally. The classic expression is found in the Book of Exodus, in words revealed to Moses, and quoted at the heading of this chapter:

> The LORD, the LORD, / a God merciful and gracious, / slow to anger, / and abounding in steadfast love and faithfulness, / keeping steadfast love for the thousandth generation, / forgiving iniquity and transgression and sin, / yet by no means clearing the guilty, / but visiting the iniquity of the parents upon the children / and the children's children, / to the third and the fourth generation. (Exod 34:6–7; cf. Ps 103:8)

This is a way of affirming the boundless nature of God's mercy. It extends to generation after generation. God's mercy and love know no boundaries and never end.

THE PSALMS

To carry our analysis further, we turn to the prayer life of Israel. Ever mindful of their own failure to live up to the law of their God, Israel often prayed for God's mercy and expected to receive it. Five examples follow:

> Be mindful of your mercy, O Lord, / and of your steadfast love, / for they have been from of old. / Do not remember the sins of my youth or my transgressions; / according to your steadfast love remember me, / for your goodness' sake, O Lord! (Ps 25:6–7)

> Do not, O Lord, withhold / your mercy from me; / let your steadfast love and your faithfulness / keep me safe forever. (40:11)

> Be merciful to me, O God, be merciful to me, / for in you my soul takes refuge; / in the shadow of your wings I will take refuge, / until the destroying storms pass by. (57:1)

> Answer me, O Lord, for your steadfast love is good; / according to your abundant mercy, turn to me. / Do not hide your face from your servant, / for I am in distress—make haste to answer me. (69:16–17)

> Bless the Lord, O my soul, / and all that is within me, / bless his holy name. / Bless the Lord, O my soul, / and do not forget all his benefits— / who forgives all your iniquity, / who heals all your diseases, / who redeems your life from the Pit, / who crowns you with steadfast love and mercy, / who satisfies you with good as long as you live / so that your youth is renewed like the eagle's. (103:1–5)

Scholars class several of these psalms as "individual laments." They express the sentiments of individuals in dire circumstances who reach out to God because of God's merciful reputation. But they can also express the sentiments of the entire people as a community. Notice that, in these samples of Israel's prayer, we see the connection between mercy and love that we referenced in the first chapter. Mercy is based upon God's steadfast love. God's constancy, fidelity, and permanent goodness are what gave Israel hope that God would be merciful to them, whether in times of their transgression or in times of distress or suffering.

An even more striking expression comes in the most explicit of the penitential psalms, which we briefly recalled earlier. The Church understandably uses this psalm weekly (Friday morning prayer) in the Liturgy of the Hours. Attributed to King David after his adultery with Bathsheba and the murder of her husband, he prays,

> Have mercy on me, O God, / according to your steadfast love; / according to your abundant mercy / blot out my transgressions. / Wash me thoroughly from my iniquity, / and cleanse me from my sin. / For I know my transgressions, / and my sin is ever before me. / Against you, you alone, have I sinned, / and done what is evil in your sight, / so that you are justified in your sentence / and blameless when you pass judgment. (51:1–4)

These words obviously connect David's request for mercy with acknowledgment of his own guilt. He asks for mercy from God, knowing that he does not deserve it, yet expecting that God will take pity on and forgive him. Given the abhorrent nature of his sin, this prayer may seem like an act of hubris. But it is a preeminent expression of confidence in the mercy of God, despite David's spectacular personal failures. No wonder Pope Francis calls it the "Magnificat of mercy."

Two other aspects of the psalms are noteworthy regarding the theme of mercy. One is that the Psalmist often makes a connection between the mercy or steadfast love of God and the obedient servants who are worthy of receiving this mercy because they remain faithful to God's commandments. Psalm 103, for example, declares,

> But the steadfast love of the LORD is from everlasting to everlasting / on those who fear him, / and his righteousness to children's children, / to those who keep his covenant / and remember to do his commandments. (103:17–18)

The expression of "fear" of the LORD in this context is the wisdom-tinged ideal of proper awe and respect that is due to God, not fearful anxiety. (Remember the wisdom adage: "The fear of the LORD is the beginning of wisdom" [Prov 1:7, au. trans.].) In this regard, we could also cite Psalm 119, an acrostic hymn (that is, it follows the Hebrew alphabet) and the longest psalm in the Bible, which offers a profound meditation on God's law or instruction (Heb. *torah*). It invokes the mercy and steadfast love of God precisely so that the Psalmist can be faithful to God's commandments (Ps 119:88–90).

A second aspect concerns the connection with human sinfulness. Even in psalms that praise God's mercy and steadfast love, there is acknowledgment that human beings all too often do not deserve to be treated with such kindness because of their perpetual sinfulness. Nonetheless, the Psalmist prays that God will continue to look kindly upon him. Psalm 103, once more, provides an excellent example of this aspect.

> The LORD is merciful and gracious, / slow to anger and abounding in steadfast love. / He will not always accuse, / nor will he keep his anger forever. / He does not deal with us according to our sins, / nor repay us according to our iniquities. / For as the heavens are high above the earth, / so great is his steadfast love toward those who fear him; / as far as the east is from the west, / so far he

> removes our transgressions from us. / As a father has compassion for his children, / so the LORD has compassion for those who fear him. (103:8–13)

Not only does this psalm show confidence in the mercy of God despite the pray-ers' sins, but it also shows the tender image of God acting as a compassionate father who cares for his children—an image that Jesus invokes in the Gospels on several occasions (see Luke 6:36; Matt 6:14, 26).

So, in the prayer of Israel, we see both affirmation of God's mercy and confidence that God will apply it liberally to a people who do not always deserve it. This confidence reaches its apex in the great hymn of praise of God as Creator and Redeemer. Its refrain echoes throughout the psalm like a mantra:

> O give thanks to the LORD, for he is good,
> *for his steadfast love* [= mercy] *endures forever.*
> O give thanks to the God of gods,
> *for his steadfast love endures forever.*
> O give thanks to the Lord of lords,
> *for his steadfast love endures forever;*
> who alone does great wonders,
> *for his steadfast love endures forever.*
>
> (Ps 136:1–4)

THE PROPHETS

The psalms reflect Israel's liturgical and prayer life, and so contain an important understanding about God's mercy. But we also need to say a word about the Old Testament prophets in relation to mercy, since their role in the Bible is prominent as well. Here again, we encounter a frequent misconception.

Many people associate the Old Testament prophets solely with a message of "fire and brimstone." According to this understanding, prophets harangued people for their failure to keep

God's covenant and, consequently, often pronounced judgment or impending doom. Even today, the modern notion of "prophet," or taking a "prophetic" stance, usually means making stern judgments about injustices, and boldly proclaiming anti-institutional messages intended to bring people to their senses. This scenario is not entirely false, for the classical prophets of the Old Testament (Isaiah, Jeremiah, Ezekiel, Hosea, Amos, etc.) did often proclaim God's judgment upon Israel and Judah,[5] especially for their failure to keep faith in the God of the covenant who had kept faith with them. But this is only one half of their story.

The other aspect of the prophets, less often emphasized, was their message of God's mercy. As spokesmen[6] for God, their duty was always first and foremost to proclaim God's Word. Their message was not their own. Many times, even sometimes in surprising circumstances, that message was one of mercy, compassion, tenderness, and forgiveness. We will take just a few examples.

At the outset, two prophetic passages demonstrate an orientation toward mercy. Jeremiah, for instance, the seventh-century prophet of the exile, receives the following message from God:

> Go, and proclaim these words toward the north, and say: / Return, faithless Israel, / says the LORD. / I will not look on you in anger, / for I am merciful, / says the LORD; / I will not be angry forever. (Jer 3:12)

God's Word—"I will not be angry *forever*"—gives us an important clue to the prophetic message. The prophets were not, we might say, "soft on crime." Their message acknowledged people's failures to live up to God's commandments, and especially the covenant. There was real evil in Israel's actions. The people of Israel often did not fulfill their obligations. This leads to God's righteous anger and subsequent possible punishment. But God affirms through Jeremiah: "I will not be angry forever," indicating that there are limits to God's just anger. He can relent.

Another prophetic passage pronounces the conviction that God is indeed merciful, but it does so in the context of calling people to repentance. It is a passage Christians use at the beginning of the season of Lent.

> Yet even now, says the LORD, / return to me with all your heart, / with fasting, with weeping, and with mourning; / rend your hearts and not your clothing. / Return to the LORD, your God, / for he is gracious and merciful, / slow to anger, and abounding in steadfast love, / and relents from punishing. (Joel 2:12–13)

Joel thus couples the exhortation to repent with the formulaic affirmation that God is "gracious and merciful, slow to anger, and abounding in steadfast love, and relents from punishing." God's merciful demeanor, then, does not let us off the hook of conversion. We are still invited, nay, exhorted, to change our ways and mold our lives according to God's ways.

Yet another prophetic passage points to the connection between God's mercy and our obligation to extend kindness and aid to those around us who are in need. This aspect ties God's mercy intimately to the call for social justice.[7] The Book of the prophet Zechariah, for instance, contains this passage:

> "Thus says the LORD of hosts: Render true judgments, show kindness and mercy to one another; do not oppress the widow, the orphan, the alien, or the poor; and do not devise evil in your hearts against one another." (Zech 7:9–10)

If mercy is a gift freely given by God, we are nonetheless always called to be merciful to those in need. In the Bible, the threefold expression "widow, orphan, stranger [NRSV 'alien']" is the standard cipher for all those in need. They are the most vulnerable in society (see Deut 10:17–18; 24:19–20; Ps 146:9; Isa 1:17; Jer 7:5–6).

Mercy and the Vulnerable

Before proceeding, these passages from Zechariah and related texts that talk of the vulnerable or the needy warrant a brief digression. It concerns an aspect of social justice that is imbedded in the concept of mercy. One cannot overestimate the importance in ancient Israel of care for those on the margins, seen primarily through the threefold category of the orphan, the widow, and the stranger. It is at one and the same time charity, mercy, and justice. The rationale for paying attention to these categories, with special reference to the "stranger" (Heb. *gēr*; sometimes translated "resident alien," "sojourner," or "foreigner") is that the people of Israel themselves were once resident aliens (Deut 10:19). Their very prototype as the "resident alien" (*immigrant,* in our language) was their ancestor Abraham (Gen 12:10; 23:4), whom God called to relocate to a foreign land. Their own displacement and vulnerability was particularly recalled as well in their sojourn in Egypt (Gen 47:4; Exod 23:9). As their ancestors of old, Israel remained forever, in a sense, "resident aliens," admitted in an ancient Hebrew "credo" (Deut 26:5–10). Thus, their own status as immigrants mandated that they treat other aliens in their midst with the same acceptance they expected and received throughout their history. The Book of Leviticus reinforces this point even more explicitly: "The alien who resides with you shall be to you as the citizen among you; you shall love the alien as yourself, for you were aliens in the land of Egypt" (19:34).

The connection between strangers and the other two categories—orphans and widows—is made clear in several texts. One example is from Exodus:

> You shall not wrong or oppress a resident alien, for you were aliens in the land of Egypt. You shall not abuse any widow or orphan. If you do abuse them, when they

> cry out to me, I will surely heed their cry; my wrath will burn, and I will kill you with the sword, and your wives shall become widows and your children orphans. (22:21–24 LXX)

Consequently, part of the ethical demand, which the prophets reiterated, was care for these persons who, because of circumstances, find themselves particularly vulnerable to abuse and mistreatment. In the ancient world, widows, orphans, and strangers needed special protection. They were three classes of people whose vulnerability in society was most precarious. Without a husband, widows had no source of income. Without parents, orphans had no protection and were libel to exploitation. Without a stable residency, strangers or immigrants were vulnerable to mistreatment and prejudice. Notice, too, that the Old Testament does not stigmatize or attempt to judge the reasons why people find themselves in such dire straits. The state of their existence is what is emphasized. All three categories symbolized the most vulnerable in society. Notice in the Exodus text just cited that there is a not-so-subtle threat: If you don't treat these people properly, you yourself may end up just as vulnerable. You could become exactly like them. So Israel's concept of mercy (here we can also speak of charity) could carry a strong ethical tinge of social justice because God ultimately is at one and the same time merciful and just. No wonder the Old Testament speaks often of the importance of protecting these minorities!

No great imagination is needed to see that this message has pertinence even today. The twenty-first century has witnessed unprecedented numbers of displaced persons and seemingly endless migration, largely because of conflicts, wars, persecution, and hatred. Many have become "refugees," fleeing terror and seeking some hope for their lives. In such a context, the prophetic voice that urged mercy on the most vulnerable in society in ancient Israel can really hit home. The quality of our treatment of such persons is on the line.

God's prophetic Word comes back to haunt: welcome the stranger, for one day you may find yourself in the same circumstance.

More Prophetic Voices

This relevant digression aside, we turn to another prophetic example of mercy, the eighth-century-BCE prophet Hosea. God instructed Hosea to marry a woman of ill repute, which would end up being an occasion for a divine message. Hosea promptly found himself in a marriage with an unfaithful wife, Gomer (Hos 1:3; yes, that is her name!). So bad is her reputation that she is referred to several times as a whore. But she bears Hosea a son and a daughter whose names are symbolic of God's intentions to bring judgment on Israel.

God's Word then comes to Hosea to say that he is to use this experience of an unfaithful marriage partner to announce a message to Israel (the Northern Kingdom). While the divine message includes a strong call to repentance for Israel's infidelity (Hos 2:1–13), modeled obviously after the human experience of unfaithfulness, the message also contains a surprising promise on God's part. God's Word pronounced by the prophet foretells of God's faithful reaching out to embrace Israel like a husband embraces an unfaithful wife, to lure her back to a loving relationship.

> Therefore, I will now allure her, / and bring her into the wilderness, / and speak tenderly to her....
>
> I will make for you a covenant on that day with the wild animals, the birds of the air, and the creeping things of the ground; and I will abolish the bow, the sword, and war from the land; and I will make you lie down in safety. And I will take you for my wife forever; I will take you for my wife in righteousness and in justice, in steadfast love, and in mercy. I will take you for my wife in faithfulness; and you shall know the LORD....
>
> And I will have pity on Lo-ruhamah (Heb. "no pity"), / and I will say to Lo-ammi (Heb. "not my people"),

"You are my people"; / and he shall say, "You are my God." (Hos 2:14, 18–20, 23)

Through the words of the prophet Hosea in this combination of poetic and narrative text, God acts like a generous and forgiving husband who will gently persuade (or perhaps "seduce") his unfaithful wife to come back. The text employs puns in Hebrew that symbolize the turnabout that God's steadfast love and mercy will establish. The verb "I will have pity" is from the Hebrew root *rḥm*, as is the expression "Lo-ruhamah." So the reversal is exact. God's pity will touch the pitiful one. Mercy will reverse non-mercy. Note well the language God uses through the prophet to emphasize that God is the one bringing about this dramatic change: "I will take you for my wife in righteousness and in justice, in steadfast love, and in mercy. I will take you for my wife in faithfulness." In this instance, what would seemingly be a hopeless situation is shown to be an opportunity for God to show undeserved and unexpected mercy and kindness.

We do not know, unfortunately, the outcome of Hosea's marital situation. But we do know that the story of God's ongoing mercy continued in the history of Israel. It is also none other than Jesus of Nazareth who, in Matthew's Gospel, draws attention to Hosea's message of mercy in contexts criticizing the Jewish leaders' opposition to his teaching and merciful actions. Twice, Jesus quotes Hosea: "Go and learn what this means, 'I desire mercy, not sacrifice'" (Matt 9:13; 12:7; see Hos 6:6). Jesus certainly took Hosea's prophetic message of God's mercy to heart. He invokes it to remind the Jewish leaders that they should be less condemning and more merciful.

Hosea may seem like a "mild" prophet, given his merciful message. But even a prophet like Amos, another eighth-century prophet to Israel, whose message seems unremittingly negative and judgmental, contains vestiges of mercy. Amos is the quintessential stern prophet whose "word of God" condemns those who profit from the poor, and he threatens punishment because of it. Amos exclaims,

> Thus says the LORD: / For three transgressions of Israel, / and for four, I will not revoke the punishment; / because they sell the righteous for silver, / and the needy for a pair of sandals— / they who trample the head of the poor into the dust of the earth, / and push the afflicted out of the way. (2:6–7; also 5:11)

Strong words to be sure. Even more impressive is the Lord's refusal to accept any offerings, which were a prominent feature of Jewish temple worship, and were generally a means to atone for their injustice.

> I hate, I despise your festivals, / and I take no delight in your solemn assemblies. / Even though you offer me your burnt offerings and grain offerings, / I will not accept them; / and the offerings of well-being of your fatted animals / I will not look upon. / Take away from me the noise of your songs; / I will not listen to the melody of your harps. / But let justice roll down like waters, / and righteousness like an ever-flowing stream. (Amos 5:21–24; cf. Mic 6:6–8)

But just when you think you have caught Amos's stern message, along comes a passage with two consecutive visions that offer a more nuanced view of God's intentions. One threatens punishment through a plague of locusts who will devour the crops and bring on famine; the other threatens judgment by a huge conflagration.

> This is what the Lord GOD showed me: he was forming locusts at the time the latter growth began to sprout.... When they had finished eating the grass of the land, I

> said, / "O Lord GOD, forgive, I beg you! / How can Jacob stand? / He is so small!" / The LORD relented concerning this; / "It shall not be," said the LORD. (7:1–3)

> This is what the Lord GOD showed me: the Lord GOD was calling for a shower of fire, and it devoured the great deep and was eating up the land. Then I said, / "O Lord GOD, cease, I beg you! / How can Jacob stand? / He is so small!" / The LORD relented concerning this; / "This also shall not be," said the Lord GOD. (7:4–6)

These two texts essentially testify to God's capacity to relent on his threats of doom. Israel (Jacob) is too tiny, implying helplessness. This people is like a little child! Sometimes God can be moved with pity not to carry out the just punishment his own chosen people deserve.

This tendency toward mercy may well have been disconcerting for some prophets. One example is Jonah, who is not one of the classical prophets but who represents a prophetic figure. The Book of Jonah is included among the twelve "minor prophets" of the Old Testament, although it does not really have many characteristics of a prophetic book. It is rather a humorous tale told of a reluctant prophet who tries to flee his prophetic call and ends up in the belly of a great fish. Eventually, he is spewed out on land and, unable to flee from his obligation to call the great foreign city of Nineveh to conversion, he reluctantly goes and preaches his message.

Then, awaiting to see what would befall the evil city—for he is convinced they will never repent—he goes a short distance, builds a little booth to provide some shade, and sits down to watch the fireworks from afar. Astonishingly, the people of Nineveh repent! Humans and animals alike, from the king down to the cattle, put on sackcloth, sit in ashes, proclaim a fast, and say, "Who knows? God may relent and change his mind; he may turn from his fierce anger, so that we do not perish" (Jonah 3:9)! The text does not hold back about Jonah's displeasure at this unexpected development:

> But this was very displeasing to Jonah, and he became angry. He prayed to the LORD and said, "O LORD! Is not this what I said while I was still in my own country? That is why I fled to Tarshish at the beginning; *for I knew that you are a gracious God and merciful, slow to anger, and abounding in steadfast love, and ready to relent from punishing*. And now, O LORD, please take my life from me, for it is better for me to die than to live." (4:1–3)

Notice the italicized words in Jonah's prayer. Just as the words of the people of Nineveh hint at the possible mercy of God, despite their deserving just punishment, so do Jonah's words admit that he feared this mercy from the very beginning. He *knew* that God was merciful. Perhaps he thought that his work as a prophet would amount to nothing if Nineveh repented and God relented.

Although we have only treated the prophets selectively here, the material is sufficient to show that they understood that God was, at heart, very merciful. Overall, the teaching of the prophets is complex, a mixture of threats, judgment, and mercy. As vehicles of God's own Word, they could be both stern and flexible. They could pronounce God's righteous judgment, or they could affirm God's merciful tendency to change his mind, to relent from the dire consequences of Israel's infidelities to the covenant.

ADDITIONAL OLD TESTAMENT PERSPECTIVES

The previous material presents the bulk of the teaching from the Old Testament on mercy. But before concluding this chapter, we should at least note that this teaching had a broader impact on other parts of the Old Testament. The wisdom literature, for instance, picks up on the theme of mercy at least on occasion and affirms the merciful nature of the God of Israel. An example is from the Book of Wisdom: "But you [God] are merciful (*eleeis*) to all, for you can do all things, and you overlook people's sins, so that they may repent (*metanoian*)" (Wis 11:23). This clearly connects the mercy of God with the expectation that human beings also repent of their sins, a theme to which we drew attention earlier. The passage uses the classic biblical vocabulary for both concepts (Gk. *eleō* "have mercy" and Gk. *metanoia* "repentance").

Other wisdom texts also draw attention to God's mercy (e.g., Sir 48:20), and one text labels God the "Merciful One" (Sir 50:19; Gk. *eleēmonos*). What is noteworthy about these texts is that the wisdom literature does not usually have a strong "theological" perspective. That is, it does not concern itself overly with salvation history and the message of God's activity in the world. It is largely the literature of collective *human* wisdom, containing a library of ethical teachings and sage advice for surviving in a complex and seductive world. Yet even the sages of Israel recognized and affirmed God's mercy.

At least one text in the wisdom literature also connects human mercy with the lawful keeping of God's commandments, a teaching we also noted earlier. "The merciful lend to their neighbors; / by holding out a helping hand they keep the commandments" (Sir 29:1). Human mercy is thus associated with observing God's laws.

Some of the later historical books of the Old Testament also refer, if briefly, to the mercy of God. Second Maccabees, for instance, has several passages that explicitly affirm God as merciful (2 Macc 8:29; 11:9; 13:12). One text connects God's mercy with justice, something to which we drew attention earlier (2 Macc 1:24; God is "just and merciful"). A related book, First Maccabees, also calls King David "merciful" (1 Macc 2:57), in the context of recounting the virtuous deeds of some of Israel's ancestors. The passage does not make it clear exactly *how* David was merciful, since no rationale is given, but the affirmation is clear. David thus provides an example of human mercy.

The Book of Tobit, numbered among the historical books, is a fictional narrative that tells a marvelous story of personal faith and how God mysteriously intervenes in human affairs. Several times throughout the Book of Tobit, the author affirms that God is ultimately merciful (3:11; 8:17; 11:17).

The point here is that these additional Old Testament references do not move in a different direction from what we outlined earlier. Rather, the perspective shows a uniformity in the biblical testimony. The Old Testament broadly affirms God's merciful nature and ties to the divine identity an expectation for humans to exercise mercy as well.

SUMMARY

This brief survey may be selective, but it leads to an inevitable conclusion. It shows that, contrary to promoting merely a violent and vengeful God, the Old Testament, too, portrays God's merciful and loving nature. From the Pentateuch to the prophets, from the historical books to the psalms and the wisdom literature, the Old Testament shows a God who is filled with tender-loving mercy. If he does not tolerate evil well and certainly threatens just punishment on those who do evil deeds, the God of the Old Testament is nonetheless a merciful One, who time and again gives people another opportunity to change their ways. This God is one and the same as the heavenly Father described by Jesus of Nazareth. From the "big picture" to minute details, the Old Testament's predominately recurring theme is that God's mercy ultimately tempers God's just judgment.

REFLECTION QUESTIONS

1. Why do people often assume that God in the Old Testament is One of justice and vengeance and not of mercy? How would you respond to such an assertion?

2. Can you identify three ways in which God in the Old Testament is portrayed as merciful? How do these characteristics match your own image of God?
3. What was the focus of the classical prophets of the Old Testament? Where does mercy fit into their overall message?
4. In what way(s) can you make the words of the psalms your own prayer? What sentiments from the psalms do you find most attractive? Why?
5. How do you interpret Hosea's use of his own marital experience as a vehicle for God's message? Is he too lenient, or weak, or tolerant toward his unfaithful spouse? Why or why not?

CHAPTER 3

JESUS, "THE FACE OF THE FATHER'S MERCY"

A NEW TESTAMENT PERSPECTIVE

> *As [Jesus] went ashore, he saw a great crowd; and he had compassion for them, because they were like sheep without a shepherd; and he began to teach them many things.* (Mark 6:34)

Jesus as a merciful figure probably seems self-evident, at least to Christians. The opening biblical quotation shows that Jesus "had compassion" on the people, "for they were like sheep without a shepherd." The first line of Pope Francis's own "bull of indiction" proclaiming the Year of Mercy begins with the outright claim, "Jesus Christ is the face of the Father's mercy" (*MV* 1), which is affirmed as a kind of summary of the New Testament perspective on mercy. But what do we really know of Jesus' quality of mercy from the New Testament? As the main "window" into the New Testament, this chapter examines this question using the canonical Gospels, with some added materials from elsewhere in the New Testament. Given that Luke has a special concentration on this theme, however, we will delay consideration of this Gospel until the next chapter.

FINDING THE PROPER IMAGE OF JESUS

Let's begin with two images. In the Basilica of the Shrine of the Immaculate Conception in Washington, DC, there is, in the dome above the sanctuary, a magnificent and imposing mosaic of Christ as the Judge on the last day. He is a stern, muscular figure, with penetrating eyes staring down on all who gaze at him. Frankly, when I first saw the image many years ago, I found it almost frightening. He seemed a fearsome judge, someone strict and unbending.

Although this image can be imposing, by contrast, I often come across images of Jesus in some contemporary contexts that make him out to be almost a milquetoast kind of figure[1]—unassertive, with dreamy eyes, long flowing hair, and a look that is just a bit too saccharine. Although some might find in these contemporary images of Jesus a soft and maybe even effeminate figure, it is nevertheless an image that appeals to many people, especially those who emphasize the importance of a personal relationship with Jesus, as in "I have a friend in Jesus."

Both images can be defended from the gospel portraits, which are certainly varied. Yet, when discussing the mercy of Jesus, we must be careful of caricature. Jesus is neither the harsh judge nor a pushover. The merciful Jesus falls somewhere in-between.

ACTIONS SPEAK LOUDER THAN WORDS

The teaching of Jesus on mercy should, above all, be seen in the context of his actions throughout his public ministry, because actions speak louder than words. All four Gospels portray Jesus as a person who performed "miracles" (lit. "mighty deeds" in the Synoptic

Gospels; called "signs" in John) and who reached out to people in need. A few examples suffice to illustrate this point.

At the beginning of his public ministry, Jesus engaged in healings and exorcisms. He immediately heals a man with an unclean spirit (Mark 1:21–28), which the Gospel of Mark labels "a new teaching—with authority" (1:27), contrasting Jesus' exercise of this power with the limp authority of the scribes. On many occasions, the Gospels explain Jesus' actions as being motivated by being "filled with compassion" or "moved with pity." The Greek expressions (e.g., *splanchnizomai,* "have compassion or pity") behind these translations connote profound human emotions, feelings that lie deep in the human experience of empathy (Matt 9:36; 14:14; 15:32; 20:34; Mark 6:34; 8:2; etc.). Interestingly, the verb used of Jesus in the Gospels is usually restricted to God in the Septuagint, implying that Jesus acts in the same compassionate manner as God described in the Old Testament.

The Synoptic Gospels record more than twenty-five miracles of Jesus (not counting parallel accounts of the same event) that show his desire to respond to human suffering and need with compassion. One thinks, for example, of various healings, like the demoniac (Mark 1:23–26; Luke 4:33–35), Peter's mother-in-law (Mark 1:30–31; Matt 8:14–15; Luke 4:38–39), the paralytic (Mark 2:3–12; Matt 9:2–7; Luke 5:18–25), and the woman with the long-term hemorrhage (Mark 5:25–34; Matt 9:20–22; Luke 8:43–48). There are also exorcism stories in which Jesus expels demons believed to be the cause of human suffering, such as the Gerasene demoniac (Mark 5:1–15; Matt 8:28–34; Luke 8:27–35), the boy possessed by a demon (Mark 9:17–29; Matt 17:14–18), and the mute demoniac (Matt 9:32–33), among others. Jesus even was reputed to have raised the dead, both to demonstrate his power over life and death and to respond to the sorrow of those left behind, such as Jairus's daughter (Mark 5:22–42; Matt 9:18–25; Luke 8:41–56), the widow of Nain (Luke 7:11–15), or his own friend Lazarus (John 11:1–44). The Gospels preserve some of these miracle stories in artificially constructed chapters (e.g., Matt 8—9), but most are scattered throughout the public ministry of Jesus and demonstrate his compassionate and merciful ministry toward suffering humanity.

Even the Gospel of John, which tends to emphasize Jesus' majesty as the cosmic Word-made-flesh, sometimes shows this more emotional side of Jesus as one who reaches out to people in their suffering. When his friend Lazarus falls ill and he delays his trip despite the urgent request of Lazarus's sisters to come heal him, Jesus arrives late, only to find Lazarus dead and buried. Upon seeing the sorrow of Lazarus's sister, Mary, Jesus himself becomes "deeply troubled" (Gk. *tarrassō*) and indeed "weeps" (Gk. *dakryō*; see John 11:34–35). In this instance, the first verb is used figuratively to indicate deep inner emotion, almost turmoil, while the second—used only once in the New Testament—literally refers to weeping. In both instances, Jesus is obviously emotionally moved with profound feelings. Only then does he raise Lazarus from the grave as testimony to his power as "the resurrection and the life" (John 11:25).

One could multiply the gospel examples, but the point is clear. Jesus' actions showed him to be both compassionate and merciful to those in need. This reputation also had the effect of emboldening people to ask Jesus for favors. On several occasions, as Jesus passes by, people cry out to him, "Lord, have mercy" (Matt 9:27; 15:22; 17:15; 20:30–31; Mark 10:47–48), the same expression that finds a life in Christian liturgy when sinners cry out to the Lord for mercy (Gk. *Kyrie, eleison*). Clearly, Jesus had a reputation for showing mercy to people in need or they would not have appealed to him for merciful actions.

MERCY AND THE AUTHORITY TO FORGIVE SINS

There is another essential aspect to this gospel portrait. The miracles of Jesus are not simply reactions to human suffering. Some of these stories are tied to the individuals not only being trapped by their physical suffering but also by their spiritual malaise. This condition is just as debilitating. When Jesus heals people of their malady, especially when he is criticized for being kind to known sinners, his response is more pointed. To the recipients of his mercy, he adds a comment and an injunction, with words like these: "your faith has saved you; now go and sin no more" (see John 5:14; cf. Matt 9:2; Mark 2:5). This becomes even more apparent in the contexts where Jesus' authority is questioned. He makes it clear that his power to heal includes, and perhaps is even primarily oriented toward, the forgiveness of sins (Matt 9:6; Mark 2:10). That is the biggest mercy of all, having sinfulness wiped away, with a new chance to begin living a righteous life again.

This added dimension is important, for it combats a common error of current thought that Jesus' actions of mercy, love, and tenderness do not include a call for a change of behavior. Yes, Jesus forgave sins; yes, he healed the sick; but he always beckoned people to repent and "sin no more." This reminds me of a billboard alongside a road in the southern United States that announced a message that basically said, "God loves you just the way you are. But he loves you too much to leave you that way." Being touched by Jesus' mercy also means being open to the grace of transformation.

We should notice another important detail, however. Jesus does not wait for people to change their lives (what we can properly call "conversion") before offering them mercy. This is perhaps Saint Paul's great insight that God's mercy reached out to us without waiting for our reform: "God proves his love for us in that while we still were sinners Christ died for us" (Rom 5:8). But neither does Jesus let us off the hook, so to speak, just because he heals us and has saved us. Jesus wants people to be whole in every sense of the term, physically, emotionally, mentally, spiritually. His mercy is thus holistic.

THE TEACHING OF JESUS

Beyond the miracles, Jesus' ministry included teaching, and he shared his ministerial authority with his disciples. His teaching indicates that he intended his followers to exhibit these same qualities of mercy, compassion, and outreach to those in need. Apart from passages that show he shared his power to heal with his disciples (e.g., Matt 10:1; Mark 3:15), his teaching in word also shows his orientation toward mercy.

The Sermon on the Mount, for example, where Jesus pronounces a blessing on the merciful: "Blessed are the merciful, for they will receive mercy" (Matt 5:7), clearly connects the reception of mercy with a merciful attitude toward others. The amount of mercy we receive may well depend upon how much we are willing to dole out, not a comforting thought if we tend to be stingy with our mercy. Is this not the meaning of another famous passage, which is the hallmark of Christian faith? The Our Father says explicitly, "forgive us our debts, / as we also have forgiven our debtors" (Matt 6:12). The Letter of James says likewise: "For judgment will be without mercy to anyone who has shown no mercy; mercy triumphs over judgment" (Jas 2:13).

Matthew's Gospel also makes clear that Jesus made mercy a centerpiece of his ministry. Twice, Jesus invokes a passage from the prophet Hosea that proclaims, "I desire mercy, not sacrifice" (Matt 9:13; 12:7; Hos 6:6), a passage to which we drew attention in chapter 2 because of the amazing story of Hosea. Moreover, Jesus rails against religious leaders who would burden people, or weigh them down, rather than alleviate their obligations (Matt 23:4), all in the name of religious observance. Even religious obligation does not overshadow mercy. Jesus' message, then, as well as his actions embody the essence of mercy that we found characteristic of God in chapter 2.

MERCY AND FORGIVENESS INEXTRICABLY LINKED

Jesus' actions and teachings on mercy are not merely aspects of his unique personality or desire. The Gospels also show that he expected his followers actively to engage in similar gestures. A passage from Matthew's Gospel illustrates the point well. Peter, the sometimes-brash spokesman for the Twelve, asks Jesus a seemingly simple question, one for which he may have been seeking a simple answer. "Lord, if another member of the church sins against me, how often should I forgive him? As many as seven times?" (Matt 18:21).

Frankly, Peter's suggested response of "seven times" sounds very generous, considering that many people would not forgive an error perhaps more than once. Jesus' response, however, is startling: "Not seven times, but, I tell you, seventy-seven times" (Matt 18:22).[2] The fact that there is likely an allusion to a Genesis story of Lamech's limitless vengeance (Gen 4:24 LXX) makes it even more likely that the meaning is for limitless forgiveness.

Furthermore, to show that forgiveness is not merely Jesus' attitude but should be that of his disciples, Jesus proceeds to offer them the parable of the unforgiving servant (Matt 18:23–35). It describes in raw detail the generosity of a "king" (also later called "master") in forgiving the indebtedness of a servant who owed a huge amount, who then turns around and demands repayment of miniscule amounts from fellow servants. Calling him a "wicked servant," the master then asks, using the standard Greek verb for "having mercy" (*eleō*): "Should you not have had mercy (Gk. *eleēsai*) on your fellow slave, as I had mercy (Gk. *ēleēsai*) on you?" (v. 33). In anger, he then sends the servant away to severe punishment. Jesus concludes, "So my heavenly Father will also do to every one of you, if you do not forgive your brother or sister from your heart" (v. 35).

Jesus' illustration could not be clearer. Mercy and forgiveness—both their reception and doling out—are inextricably linked. As we are forgiven by a God whose mercy knows no bounds, so likewise are we commanded to bestow mercy on others. Pope Francis has called attention to this approach in his document proclaiming the year of mercy. His comment on this very parable is:

> Jesus affirms that mercy is not only an action of the Father, it becomes a criterion for ascertaining who his true children are. In short, we are called to show mercy because mercy has first been shown to us. (*MV* 9; see also *AL* 310)

An easily missed detail to this teaching of Jesus is that it follows a scene in which Jesus has been teaching his disciples about the nature of discipleship (Matt 18:1–20). He sets forth a pastoral way of dealing with "sinners" in the community that may reflect an actual practice in the Matthean community (vv. 15–18). It is a commonsense kind of approach. If someone sins against you, the first path should be personally to point out that individual's error. If that does not bring him around, then you are to take one or two more from the community for a confrontation. If that still does not bring the wrongdoer around, only then does Jesus say, "Tell it to the church" (v. 17), which means to bring the matter to the proper authorities. If that also fails to bring about repentance, only then does Jesus say to treat him as you would "a Gentile" or "a tax collector" (v. 17), tantamount, ironically, to making him a target for more serious evangelization!

Note the progression. One does not simply overlook transgressions, but one also does not invoke a higher authority as the first step to getting wayward community members back on the right path. Unfortunately, in many parochial situations I have encountered, some Catholics who seemingly see themselves as guardians of orthodoxy sometimes want to condemn perceived offenders before a tribunal, rather than first attempting to work with such people to address ways to resolve the situation. There is a tendency to flee to authority and to overlook the principle of subsidiarity. The Matthean community apparently took Jesus' message to heart and tried a subtler approach.

ADDITIONAL NEW TESTAMENT PERSPECTIVES

Suspending discussion of the Pauline letters for the time being—we will treat them separately in more detail in chapters 4 and 5—we turn briefly to other writings in the New Testament apart from the Gospels. If the lion's share of the New Testament perspective on mercy is found in the Gospels, especially the Synoptics, there are nonetheless other strands of the theme of mercy that extend throughout the New Testament. We draw attention to some of them here.

In general, one finds several references to mercy in greetings found at the beginning or end of some New Testament books. The theme is usually coupled with one or more prayerful wishes, such as "grace" or "peace." Two examples are:

> May mercy, peace, and love be yours in abundance. (Jude 2)

> Grace, mercy, and peace will be with us from God the Father and from Jesus Christ, the Father's Son, in truth and love. (2 John 1:3)

While such passages do not extend our understanding of the concept of mercy, they show that, in New Testament times, Christians had already made mercy a standard part of their vocabulary.

Another use of the concept appears in the Letter of James. This document, which is disguised as a letter, is a small tract of wisdom teaching. It is not surprising, then, to find Old Testament concepts used and adapted for Christian purposes. A primary example is the strong exhortation to become more merciful. James gives the following rationale:

> For where there is envy and selfish ambition, there will also be disorder and wickedness of every kind. But the wisdom from above is first pure, then peaceable, gentle, willing to yield, full of mercy (Gk. *eleous*) and good fruits, without a trace of partiality or hypocrisy. And a harvest of righteousness is sown in peace for those who make peace. (Jas 3:16–18)

This passage comes at the end of a section laying out the nature of true human wisdom. Mercy plays an important part of an ethically upright life. Where there is mercy and its attendant "fruits," one will not find jealousy and division.

A second passage from James emphasizes the importance of mercy even more strongly:

> So speak and so act as those who are to be judged by the law of liberty. For judgment will be without mercy to anyone who has shown no mercy; mercy triumphs over judgment. (2:12–13)

If you do not show mercy, you will not receive mercy! This teaching is reminiscent of Jesus' own teaching in the Sermon on the Mount and elsewhere that demands giving mercy in order to receive it (Matt 6:14–15; also 18:32–33). It is closely tied to forgiveness, as expressed in the Lord's Prayer (Matt 6:12). So, in James, we can say that we encounter a reinforcement of the gospel message that mercy is part of Christian existence.

The brief Letter of Jude makes a similar point regarding mercy. It contains an explicitly ethical message calling for mercy in various circumstances.

> But you, beloved, build yourselves up on your most holy faith; pray in the Holy Spirit; keep yourselves in the love of God; look forward to the mercy (Gk. *eleos*) of our Lord Jesus Christ that leads to eternal life. And have mercy (Gk. *eleate*) on some who are wavering; save others by snatching them out of the fire; and have mercy (Gk. *eleate*) on still others with fear, hating even the tunic defiled by their bodies. (Jude 20–23)

Particularly noteworthy here is the exhortation to have mercy on those who are wavering in their faith. Whenever persecutions arose in Christian history, there was always a temptation for some to waver in their faith or even to become apostates (i.e., deny the faith). Shusako Endo, the great Japanese novelist, described such a circumstance in seventeenth-century Japan in his novel *Silence* (1966), which Martin Scorsese made into a remarkable film of the same title in 2016. Severe persecution could lead to defections from the faith. Some Christians would look harshly upon such apostates. But Jude seemingly recognizes the danger in such situations and calls for mercy to encourage people under such stress. We notice, too, that the author speaks of the mercy that "leads to eternal life." This alludes to the mercy we receive freely from Jesus Christ. In receiving mercy, we are invited to extend it to others who find themselves in difficulty.

Another document, the Letter to the Hebrews, moves the theme of mercy in a slightly different direction. This letter is a lengthy, well-developed, sophisticated sermon on the unique image of Jesus Christ, the Eternal High Priest. It is filled with innumerable Old Testament quotations and allusions. Almost all the theology of Hebrews touches on, in one way or another, the understanding of Jesus as the great High Priest. In this context, the lessons about mercy come through with distinct emphases.

One lesson concerns the humanness of Christ as the High Priest. His exalted position is not so that he can lord it over the rest of us. On the contrary, Hebrews explains,

> Therefore he [Christ] had to become like his brothers and sisters in every respect, so that he might be a merciful (Gk. *eleēmōn*) and faithful (Gk. *pistos*) high priest in the service of God, to make a sacrifice of atonement for the sins of the people. (2:17)

This passage thus shows Christ as the merciful one who can be merciful to us precisely because he shares our own human existence. He is the High Priest chosen "from among men [NRSV 'mortals']" (Heb 5:1) who is like us in every way, "yet without sin" (Heb 4:15). As High Priest, he is in the unique position to make the proper atonement that we need for our sinfulness.

Hebrews reinforces this perspective with two other images that recall the notion of mercy by invoking various Old Testament practices, now overshadowed by the new High Priest, Jesus Christ. One is the mention of the "mercy seat" (Heb 9:5; Gk. *hilastērion*; NABRE "place of expiation"). This is a direct reference to the golden top of the ark of the covenant described in the Old Testament (see Lev 16). The ark was considered the dwelling place of God prior to the building of the temple in Jerusalem. It was also associated with the ritual for atonement done once a year on Yom Kippur by the high priest, who sprinkled the blood of sacrificial animals for the expiation of sin.

The other image is covenantal. Hebrews contains a long quotation from the prophet Jeremiah about the "new covenant," now seen fulfilled in Jesus Christ (Heb 8:8–12; Jer 31:31–34). At the end of the citation comes the following reminder, God's words spoken through the prophet Jeremiah and now taken over by the author of Hebrews:

> "For I will be merciful (Gk. *hileōs*) toward their iniquities, / and I will remember their sins no more." (Heb 8:12; see also Jer 31:34)

What the text asserts is that this passage has been fulfilled in Jesus Christ. As the new High Priest, he is now the one who brings God's mercy to fruition. He is the perfect Hight Priest making the perfect (self-)sacrifice and thus bringing about the "new covenant" already promised by Jeremiah. The viewpoint is obviously sophisticated and highly theological. It also shows how the concept of mercy continued to impact Christian theology as it reflected at length on the "Christ-event."

Another important perspective that builds on both Old and New Testament concepts comes from the First Letter of Peter. It has the appearance of a letter but is more likely a sermon whose primary theme is Christian baptism and its significance. Two passages contain important observations on mercy.

The first passage quotes the prophet Hosea, who, as we saw in chapter 2, was a prophet of God's mercy. First Peter testifies,

> Once you were not a people, / but now you are God's people; / once you had not received mercy, / but now you have received mercy. (2:10; cf. Hos 2:23)

This quotation comes at the end of a series of Old Testament citations that lead to the main point: Through the Christian community, God has fulfilled the ideal of creating a chosen people worthy of their call. Baptism has basically made of us a new chosen people, a royal priesthood, a holy nation, a people set apart (see 1 Pet 2:9). We had been left in the dark and without mercy, but now are reborn into the light by the mercy of God. The Old Testament perspective provides the firm foundation for the deeper Christian message.

The second quotation advances the Christian aspect of this mercy even further because it explicitly connects God's mercy with the new birth that has come about through the resurrection. Keep in mind that the notion of the resurrection is distinctly Christian.[3] Nothing in the Old Testament had exactly prepared the Jews for the notion of an individual resurrection as Jesus experienced, although late Judaism began to hope in a general resurrection of the dead (e.g., Dan 12:1–3, 13; 2 Macc 7:14). At the beginning of the letter, then, First Peter asserts,

> Blessed be the God and Father of our Lord Jesus Christ! By his great mercy (Gk. *eleos*) he has given us a new birth into a living hope through the resurrection of Jesus Christ from the dead. (1:3)

In this passage, the Father's gracious action of raising Jesus Christ from the dead has given those reborn in baptism cause for hope. God's mercy provides hope for new life.

While it might come as a surprise, the Gospel of John does not use the language of mercy. Instead, the emphasis is on the strongly related concept of *love*. The language of "love" (usually Gk. *agapē* and *agapaō*) is used more than 110 times in the Gospel and three Letters of John; so, it is an extensive theme. Here we can only indicate the main lines of the concept as it touches the theme of mercy. There are two principal strands to this theme in the Johannine literature.

The first strand can be called the "vertical dimension" of love. The most eloquent explanatory text from the Johannine literature is the famous verse—"For God so loved the world that he gave his only Son, so that everyone who believes in him may not perish but may have eternal life" (John 3:16). In the Johannine worldview, God sent his Son from "above" into the world "below"—light coming into our darkness—so that he could return to the Father "above," eventually taking us with him. It is essentially a vertical movement, down and up. This kind of love can only be attributed to a God whose mercy knows no bounds. To give his only begotten Son for a world filled with darkness and sin is the ultimate testimony to the gift of mercy that we have been describing. God's love is his mercy, and vice versa.

The second strand can be called the "horizontal dimension" of love. In addition to explaining God's never-ending love, John also shows Jesus issuing a new commandment to his followers. They are to "love one another as I have loved you" (John 15:12; also 13:34; 15:17; 1 John 3:11, 14; 2 John 1:5). In other words, this love received is to be shared with one another. It is the horizontal love of neighbor. Although the teaching of the Johannine literature[4] is far richer than we can expound here, this basic twofold orientation, I suggest, explains that even if the vocabulary of mercy is missing, the underlying concept is present in the overarching concept of love.

We conclude our discussion of New Testament texts with the Book of Revelation. It belongs in a category of its own. It, too, does not explicitly contain the biblical language of mercy we have been describing, yet it nevertheless contains a related message.

Keeping in mind that the main context of Revelation is the message of faithfulness under persecution, and the exhortation to remain faithful even to the point of martyrdom, what we should not lose sight of is the final victory that Revelation promises. The book concludes with a great vision of a "new heaven and new earth" embodied in the "the holy city, the new Jerusalem, coming down out of heaven from God, prepared as a bride adorned for her husband" (Rev 21:2). What such imagery implies is nothing less than a new beginning, which is due both to God's final victory over evil and to his gracious act of establishing what amounts to a new creation.

This is the ultimate "fresh start" that is part of the biblical message of mercy. We should not miss, too, that the text speaks of a new, faithful marriage (remember the imagery in Hosea): God is prepared to take this new Jerusalem as his bride, just as the renewal of the covenant had always promised. If the language of mercy is missing in Revelation, the action of mercy is not. In fact, what Revelation promises is a final act of mercy on God's part to provide us a new beginning, rooted, of course, in Christ himself, the sacrificial

"Lamb" who accomplishes the ultimate victory over evil and provides the light for the new Jerusalem (Rev 21:23).

POPE FRANCIS'S CALL FOR A JUBILEE OF MERCY

When Pope Francis issued his "bull of indiction," *Misericordiae Vultus* ("The Face of Mercy"), which established the special jubilee for mercy, it was obvious that almost every aspect of the jubilee was to be rooted in Jesus Christ. The first words of the document exemplify this: "Jesus Christ is the face of the Father's mercy.... Mercy has become living and visible in Jesus of Nazareth, reaching its culmination in him" (*MV* 1).

Both aspects of this theme of mercy should be noted. As we have emphasized before, God the Father is the embodiment of mercy. God's very nature is merciful. The second aspect is that his Son incarnates this same mercy and shares it freely in the world. Jesus' merciful nature, then, is a reflection of his Father's merciful nature; like father, like son. However, Jesus carries it one step further by asking that his disciples implement mercy in the same fashion; like master, like disciple. Indeed, the motto of the holy year was explicitly, "Merciful like the Father" (see *MV* 14). Pope Francis's document quotes many gospel passages where Jesus' actions and teachings clearly demonstrate the call to mercy. Moreover, Pope Francis invites all to follow the example of Jesus and put his teachings into practice.

Concretely, the Holy Father also gave explicit attention to the sacrament of reconciliation, especially during the season of Lent. He is aware that many Catholics have allowed the sacrament to fall into disuse; some are also fearful of it. He also points out that some confessors have not been as merciful as we are called to be, and sometimes bad experiences in the confessional have encouraged people to stay away. So, Pope Francis issues a strong appeal to confessors to do their job better:

> I will never tire of insisting that confessors be authentic signs of the Father's mercy. We do not become good confessors automatically. We become good confessors when, above all, we allow ourselves to be penitents in search of his mercy. Let us never forget that to be confessors means to participate in the very mission of Jesus to be a concrete sign of the constancy of divine love that pardons and saves....In short, confessors are called to be a sign of the primacy of mercy always, everywhere, and in every situation, no matter what. (*MV* 17)

This was a strong call to confessors to become more merciful, essentially to become more like Jesus, the face of the Father's mercy. As a priest, I personally found the advice both sage and challenging. Dealing especially with repeat sinners (aren't we all?) is not always easy. Backsliding is not an attractive characteristic. Yet the New Testament message of Jesus clearly shows that this is the attitude he had and that he called his disciples to have. The pope's vision, then, was in line with Jesus' practice.

THE ONGOING CHALLENGE

This summary of Jesus' message of mercy, in the context of the Jubilee Year of Mercy, surely has shown us that mercy is not an easy path to walk. There is a delicate balance between condemning (or at least not abetting) the evil acts that human beings do, and yet being merciful toward the perpetrators. When I was a boy, I regularly heard preached, "Condemn the sin but not the sinner." Often, though, human tendency is to condemn both. Even worse, it is always easier to see the sinfulness and failures of others than to acknowledge our own, as Jesus reminds us with the contrast of the "log" in our own eye and the splinter in our neighbor's (Matt 7:3–5). There is a thin line between being righteous and being *self*-righteous. The latter has a way of dampening mercy; the former is the honest admission that sin still raises its ugly head in the human arena. Jesus obviously walked this same path to which he called his disciples, but he found a way to be merciful while not condoning sin. If the special jubilee year invited Christians to do the same, it was with the understanding that the task is not meant only to be an exceptional one for a limited time. It is meant to be a lifelong commitment.

REFLECTION QUESTIONS

1. Do you think the image of Jesus being compassionate and merciful makes him a weak figure? Why or why not?
2. What do you understand by the expression that "Jesus is the face of the Father's mercy"? What is the relationship between Jesus' teaching and that of his heavenly Father?
3. Identify a few concrete stories in the New Testament that show Jesus to be compassionate and merciful. How do you apply these stories in your own life?
4. What is the relationship between mercy and forgiveness? How easy do you find it to forgive those who have somehow offended you?
5. How do you personally cope with the notion that one should condemn the sin but not the sinner? Is it humanly possible? How does one distinguish the two?

CHAPTER 4

LUKE, THE GOSPEL OF MERCY

Thus [God] has shown the mercy promised to our ancestors, / and has remembered his holy covenant, / the oath that he swore to our ancestor Abraham. (Luke 1:72–73, the Canticle of Zechariah)

The Year of Mercy proclaimed by Pope Francis dovetailed nicely with the liturgical year of Luke, which began on the first Sunday of Advent in November 2014 and lasted until the Feast of Christ the King at the end of November 2015. It provided a timely occasion to examine this Gospel in more depth. Luke is often rightly characterized as "the Gospel of mercy," which warranted treating this Gospel separately. In this chapter, we will explore some of the reasons for this designation.

HYMNS ON THE MERCY OF GOD

The Lukan orientation toward mercy appears early in the Gospel in the two parallel stories of the announcements of the births of John the Baptist and Jesus. The Gospel begins with the tale of the miraculous conception of John to his elderly parents, Elizabeth and Zechariah. An "angel of the Lord" (Luke 1:11) appears to the priest Zechariah during his temple duties and announces that his son will be "filled with the Holy Spirit" and "turn" the hearts of people to make them "prepared for the Lord" (vv. 15, 17). Zechariah's skepticism results in his becoming mute. The story then turns its attention to a similar scenario, this time to a young virgin named Mary, who is betrothed to Joseph. The angel Gabriel makes a similar announcement of a miraculous conception, this time not despite old age but by the action of the Holy Spirit and through no human contact.

Mary's reaction provides the first hymnic (poetic) response to God's miraculous actions. Her hymn, the Magnificat (Luke 1:46–55), speaks profoundly of the mercy of God (usually Gk. *eleos*; vv. 50, 54). It also ties mercy to God's saving action in the world—God's intervention, we might say, on behalf of the needy. God is explicitly proclaimed as "Savior" (Gk. *sōtēr*, v. 47). The hymn announces the reversal of human fortunes in this world: God casting down mighty ones and lifting up lowly ones. It praises God whose "mercy is…from generation to generation" and who always helps his chosen people Israel "in remembrance of his mercy." The entire hymn exalts God and God's merciful and saving action toward those in need. It also sets forth themes that will appear throughout the Lukan narrative, especially God's merciful outreach and God's salvation. It recounts divine justice, in which God's favor and mercy cause an unexpected reversal of fortune. God's mercy shown to Mary, the humble virgin from Nazareth, is thus emblematic of God's inherent identity as the Merciful One.

The story then returns immediately to Elizabeth and Zechariah whose neighbors and relatives, at the birth of their son, "heard that the Lord had shown his great mercy to her" (1:58). Zechariah, having confirmed his son's name as John, has his tongue loosened. He then blesses God and proclaims a hymn, called the "Benedictus"

(1:68–79), which equally draws attention to God's mercy. It affirms that God has "looked favorably on his people and redeemed them," and that God has bestowed "salvation" and redemption on the people, showing "mercy," as God has always promised their ancestors. Indeed, Zechariah proclaims "the tender mercy of our God" for bringing light into the darkness and for rescuing his people from their enemies. This text reinforces the perspective announced by Mary in the Magnificat and affirms explicitly that God's mercy brings redemption and salvation. In fact, "salvation" (Gk. *sōtēria*) is mentioned three times in the hymn (vv. 68, 71, 77), and is clearly linked to God's tender mercy (vv. 72, 78), which means God's saving help from enemies.

Using familiar biblical terminology for mercy that we analyzed in chapter 1, coupled with the related concepts of redemption and salvation, each of these hymns celebrates, in powerful and interrelated ways, God's mercy seen in the intertwined stories of John the Baptist and Jesus of Nazareth. We should also note that the concepts of mercy and salvation are not merely "pie in the sky" images. These hymns concretely reference God's merciful, saving actions in this world. God saves his people from their enemies, and he lifts up the lowly. God's mercy accomplishes "great things." This is why the faithful sing God's praises. The Church uses these hymns daily in the Liturgy of the Hours. The Benedictus occurs in morning prayer, while the Magnificat concludes evening prayer. They are like bookends of mercy consecrating each day in remembrance of God's gracious and saving actions toward his people.

JESUS' PUBLIC MINISTRY

If the first chapters of Luke orient the story of Jesus of Nazareth toward God's mercy that he embodies, then Jesus' first major action after his baptism confirms this orientation. Most scholars view the rejection at Nazareth (4:16–30) as programmatic for Luke's Gospel. It reveals how Jesus' ministry will unfold.

This familiar story, in which Jesus reads at synagogue a passage from the scroll of Isaiah (Isa 61:1–2) and pronounces its fulfillment "today" (Gk. *sēmeron*), is enlightening. We should note that Luke makes the notion of "today" and "now" a special theme in Jesus' ministry. In comparison to Mark and Matthew, Luke emphasizes that God's grace and mercy are actively present "now" in Jesus' miracles and teaching (see, e.g., 4:21; 5:26; 6:20–26; 11:3; 13:32; 19:5, 9; 23:43). This phrasing helps portray the immediacy of Jesus' ministry and likewise affirms the notion that the "kingdom [or reign] of God" is not merely in the indefinite future but can be experienced here and now. The inbreaking of God's kingdom is already evident; mercy and God's justice are seen in the ministry of Jesus. This is a Lukan teaching worth recalling in our own day when many people emphasize the kingdom (or heaven) as only a distant and future reality.

Although the word *mercy* does not occur explicitly in this passage, its content can be understood only in this light. It speaks of an anointing by the Lord's Spirit for a series of ministerial and merciful activities:

- to bring glad tidings to the poor;
- to proclaim liberty to captives;
- to give sight to the blind;
- to free the oppressed;
- to proclaim a year of favor in the Lord.

One can scarcely conceive of a broader and more concrete vision of God's mercy. And Jesus affirms that this prophetic vision is now coming to pass in his own ministry. Later, the Gospel confirms this perspective when Jesus answers the question of John the Baptist while John sits in prison. He sends his disciples to ask if Jesus is "the one who is to come" or not (7:18–19). Jesus' response is to refer to his prophetic deeds of mercy:

> The blind receive their sight, the lame walk, the lepers are cleansed, the deaf hear, the dead are raised, the poor have good news brought to them. (7:22)

This Isaian prophecy is being fulfilled in Jesus' own actions. We also remember, of course, that the scene at the synagogue in Nazareth concludes with the crowd from Nazareth becoming angry at Jesus' apparent impertinence, usurping God's merciful role; they try to throw him off a cliff. Jesus simply comments, "No prophet is accepted in the prophet's hometown" (4:24). It is a dark harbinger of the kind of opposition God's mercy in Jesus' ministry will engender.

This critical scene establishes Jesus' prophetic identity, affirms his orientation to proclaim "good news" (4:18; 7:22; Gk. *euangelizō*; the verb used in the Isaiah passage [Isa 61:1]) of God's extended mercy, and also foreshadows the difficulties he will face throughout his public ministry, which, ultimately, will lead to his suffering, death, and resurrection in Jerusalem.

ACTS OF MERCY

The forceful announcement at Nazareth leads immediately to the fulfillment of this Isaian-inspired ministry in the deeds and teachings of Jesus. While a large part of this information overlaps significantly with Mark and Matthew—the other two Synoptic Gospels—Luke nevertheless develops the story of Jesus his own way. We need not repeat here the information in the previous chapter that showed how Jesus' ministry was the embodiment of mercy. Luke, too, shows Jesus reaching out compassionately to those in need, responding to their petitions to heal them, and often relating his merciful actions to the most merciful one of all—the forgiveness of sins. Yet, Luke adds some special emphases on mercy.

One example is found in a line in the Sermon on the Plain (6:17–49), Luke's version of the more famous Matthean "Sermon on the Mount" (Matt 5—7). In the context of the teaching to love one's enemies, the Lukan Jesus reminds his hearers that God, the Most High, is "kind (Gk. *chrēstos*) to the ungrateful and the wicked" (Luke 6:35). The Greek word used here has multiple meanings but implies kind, loving, and benevolent sentiments. Then follows Jesus' admonition: "Be merciful (Gk. *oiktirmenos*), just as your Father is merciful (Gk. *oiktirmōn*)" (v. 36). These Greek words occur in the Septuagint usually in relation to God's nature, implying fullness of compassion; they always occur with the regular vocabulary of "mercy" (the root *elee-*). So Jesus clearly instructs the hearers of his sermon to become like God—full of compassion and mercy.

This is obviously different from Matthew's version: "Be perfect…as your heavenly Father is perfect" (Matt 5:48). The Greek word for "perfect" used in Matthew's passage is *teleios*, which does not mean to be without any flaws. Rather, it means to be entirely goal oriented, to ceaselessly strive for the kind of perfection that is found in God the Father but that can be so sorely lacking in the human sphere. Both the Matthean and Lukan messages are challenging; neither is easily implemented. Yet the Lukan preference for the vocabulary of kindness, compassion, and mercy puts the emphasis on values that are both ideal and possible in the human arena.

SIX SPECIAL LUKAN EXAMPLES

Another way to see Luke's attraction to the theme of mercy and compassion is to examine stories that are unique to his Gospel. Let us briefly discuss six of them.

THE GOOD SAMARITAN

The first special Lukan narrative is the beloved parable of the Good Samaritan (10:29–37). Jesus tells the parable in response to a question that, at first, may seem innocent, but in reality, is a setup after a legal scholar had sought to justify himself by observing the commandments to love God and neighbor (6:25–28). He asks Jesus a seemingly simple question, "And who is my neighbor?"

In response, Jesus tells the story of the man going down from Jerusalem to Jericho who is beset by robbers, stripped naked, beaten, and left for dead on the side of the road. A priest and a Levite, separately traveling on the same road, bypass the man. Finally, a Samaritan—despised by the Jews—happens on the poor man, treats his wounds, and takes him to an inn, offering to pay for the man's care on his way back. Jesus then asks which of the three was "neighbor" to the victim? The scholar rightly replies, "The one who showed him *mercy* (*eleos*)," to which Jesus advises, "Go and do likewise" (10:37). The startling aspect of the parable, of course, is that people normally define *neighbor* in terms of acquaintances, or people with whom we are familiar, or members of our own "group"—not despised enemies! The one who was a true neighbor was the least expected one. We should not miss the import of this message: the hated outsider (the Samaritan) not only embodies the real meaning of mercy but in effect teaches what it means to love our neighbor. The outsider's behavior becomes the ideal model of mercy. Even more importantly, notice that his mercy is, in effect, the ability to enter into the victim's suffering. He showed (Gk. *poieō*, which means "do") the poor man mercy! He empathized to the point of acting on his behalf. He accomplished mercy by his kind action of tending to the victim's dire state, even to the point of extending "credit" for his care until his return.

This story has become so well known that today we use the expression "Good Samaritan" of anyone who acts compassionately toward others. Mercy extends to anyone in need, not simply to those we favor, we like, or we prefer.

THE BARREN FIG TREE

A second unique story in Luke concerns the parable of the barren fig tree (13:6–9). While the other Gospels also contain stories of fig trees, Luke's is unique in its details. The story follows a strong passage in which Jesus recalls two tragedies, one in Galilee and one in Siloam, in which victims died horrifically (13:1–5). Jesus relates these incidents with a call to conversion. Jesus warns that his hearers could face a similar fate if they do not repent, which sounds ominous. Then he tells the parable.

In the Lukan version, the fig tree, which has not borne fruit for three years, is about to be cut down. A man has lost patience with the tree. And why not! It is taking up space; why should it "be wasting the soil"? So, he asks his gardener to cut it down. This seems reasonable, as three years implies a long time waiting. (Also, think of the rule of three—three strikes and you're out.) Surprisingly, the gardener asks the man for more patience. He asks him to leave it one more year, during which he will fertilize it and tend to it. Only then, if it does not bear fruit, it can be cut down. The message is one of undeserved reprieve. God is like the gardener with the fig tree. God's patience with sinners, in fact, is inexhaustible. Though we heard the warning sounded in the preceding lines, the more lasting message is that even the tree that does not bear good fruit (a biblical image for living righteously) can be given another chance. Good news for repeat sinners!

THE MERCY CHAPTER: LOST AND FOUND

Yet another beloved story unique to Luke's Gospel is the lengthy parable of the so-called prodigal son (15:11–32). In fact, the entire chapter 15 of Luke comprises three stories of God seeking out the lost. The other two are parallel parables of the lost sheep (15:1–7) and lost coin (15:8–10), one featuring a man and the other a woman. In the first instance, it is remarkable that a shepherd would leave ninety-nine sheep untended to go seek out one wayward animal. But that is what Jesus describes. The shepherd even "lays it on his shoulders and rejoices" (v. 5). This image was not lost on the early Christians who saw in this action a merciful shepherd. One of the earliest artistic images of Jesus the Good Shepherd is found on the walls of a catacomb and shows Jesus with a lamb draped over his shoulders.[1]

The second story is similar, but the protagonist is a woman who loses one of ten silver coins (Gk. *drachmas*) in her own house.[2] She lights a lamp and diligently searches. Upon finding it, she gathers her friends and neighbors to help her rejoice that the lost coin has been found. Jesus uses it once more as an illustration of the joy that God finds in seeking out the lost. It is mercy in action. Both little stories concern the joy that comes from finding something (or someone!) that has been lost. So, they lead well into the climactic story of the lost son.

Many artists have portrayed this story beautifully through their paintings and sculptures, most notably a famous image by Rembrandt, which has been used multiple times to symbolize the theme of mercy. The story is simple enough. A younger, perhaps impatient, son virtually insults his father by asking for his inheritance so that he can go off to a distant land and live a dissolute life. The father must have been terribly disappointed, if not devastated. Yet, after having squandered all his resources and finding himself starving and homeless, the young man comes to his senses (lit. "came to himself") and decides to return home, beg his father's forgiveness, and ask to be treated only as a hired hand, no longer a son. This he does, but when he is yet "a long way off," his father sees him—indicating the father's expectant waiting, searching the horizon—runs out to him, embraces him, and orders that he be clothed well and that a feast be prepared to celebrate his return. This angers the older son who believes he has been overlooked while his irresponsible brother is being pampered and rewarded for bad behavior. The father's pleas and assurance of love notwithstanding, the older son sulks while the father proclaims, "This brother of yours was dead and has come to life; he was lost and has been found."

The meaning is clear. God operates a lost-and-found department, precisely the place where one can be welcomed back yet again when we stray from the path of righteousness. It is a message of mercy, compassion, and love that overshadows the need for judgment and just punishment for wrongdoing.

ZACCHAEUS

The fourth example is the familiar story of Zacchaeus the tax collector (19:1–10). Short in stature, he tries in vain to see Jesus when Jesus is walking by, but the crowds are too thick. So, he climbs a sycamore tree, and when Jesus sees him, he bids him to come down, "for I must stay at your house today." Overjoyed, Zacchaeus welcomes Jesus and acknowledges that he will give half of his goods to the poor and repay fourfold anyone he has extorted. (Extortion by despised tax collectors was endemic in that era.) Jesus then pronounces the message that harks back to the beginning of Luke's narrative: "Today salvation has come to this house." The combination of "today" (*sēmeron*) and "salvation" (*sotēria*) reinforces our earlier point that Luke emphasizes the immediacy and availability of God's mercy, compassion, and even salvation. Mercy reaches out and saves again. Even a lowly and despised tax collector is deserving of mercy. Noteworthy, too, is that Jesus makes no demand on Zacchaeus. There is no call to repentance or conversion. Rather, Zacchaeus offers his own just actions in recompense for perceived wrongs, seemingly in response to Jesus' invitation to "come down" from his perch so that he can host Jesus. In a sense, Jesus' nonjudgmental stance at the outset impacts Zacchaeus's own merciful actions.

THE PHARISEE AND THE TAX COLLECTOR

Another uniquely Lukan story is the parable of the Pharisee and the tax collector (18:10–14). From one angle, it is not about mercy, as such. It is about humility and the need to rely totally on God. But we notice at the start that Jesus addresses the parable to "some who trusted in themselves that they were righteous and regarded others with contempt" (v. 9). This is the setup. The audience is arrogant and looks down on others. So Jesus tells them a parable intended to illustrate a more proper attitude. He proceeds to contrast two men who go to the temple to pray. The first, a Pharisee, haughtily touts his worth to God in his prayer by pointing out how superior he is compared to others, "or even like this tax collector" (v. 11). For his part, the tax collector stays well back, not even daring to raise his eyes toward heaven, humbly beats his breast, and prays, "God, be merciful (Gk. *hilaskomai*) to me, a sinner!" (v. 13). We have not seen the Greek verb here in our earlier discussions, but it connotes the need for expiation of sin. It is a heartfelt cry for forgiveness, for mercy, from one who honestly recognizes his sinfulness. From the punchline about humility, we see that Jesus intends this story as an example of the proper attitude for his followers. They are to recognize their sinfulness, rely on God's merciful forgiveness, and remain humble. They are also encouraged to ask for God's mercy, just as the tax collector did.

A VIEW FROM THE CROSS

Finally, one can point to Jesus' own words from the cross near the end of the Lukan narrative. After having been mistreated, scourged, mocked, and crucified, Jesus nonetheless gazes upon those who have perpetrated this evil and says, "Father, forgive them; for they do not know what they are doing" (23:34).[3] This is the kind of gratuitous mercy so characteristic of God. Jesus intercedes even for his persecutors, asking for God's mercy upon them. He also promises "Paradise" to the repentant thief who is crucified alongside him (23:43). There is no greater testimony to the mercy of God than that which is found in his Son, Jesus Christ, the Savior and Redeemer of the world.

This is ultimately Luke's great message: from beginning to end, the story of Jesus of Nazareth is one of compassion, mercy, and salvation—truly good news for all sinners willing to accept this outstretched hand of love.

WHAT ABOUT THE ACTS OF THE APOSTLES?

Readers familiar with biblical studies will no doubt wonder about how the Acts of the Apostles fits into this Lukan perspective on mercy. Acts is, after all, closely related to the Gospel of Luke (cf. Luke 1:1–4 and Acts 1:1–5). Luke-Acts is the only two-volume work in the New Testament. The primary reason that they are separated by the Gospel of John is due to the formation of the New Testament canon. From the beginning of Christianity, the Gospels took precedence because they narrate the story of Jesus of Nazareth. As the canon took shape, the four Gospels—Matthew, Mark, Luke, and John—were kept together at the beginning of the New Testament canon. Thus, Acts became separated from its first volume. It follows on John and precedes the letters of the New Testament because it tells the story of the early Church. In a sense, Acts is the natural outcome of the Gospels and Jesus' command to evangelize throughout the world, but it also rightly prepares for the letters of the New Testament that help to deepen the understanding of Jesus' message and the Christian mission.

Acts, perhaps surprisingly, does not utilize the traditional language of mercy we have been explaining, except for one related word. That word is the noun *almsgiving* (*eleēmosynē*), which occurs eight times in Acts (3:2, 3, 10, etc.) and comes from the same Greek root as *merciful* (*elee-*). What this connotes, however, is not an attitude or feeling. Rather, it is an explicit and specific act of mercy or kindness—giving alms to the poor and the needy. It is essentially a charitable deed. In relation to this word, we should also note that the Septuagint usually uses it to translate the Hebrew word for "righteousness" or "justice" (*ts^e^daqah*). This may imply more than charity; it could also suggest an obligation (Isa 1:27; 59:16; Pss 24:5; 33:5).

The lack of the traditional vocabulary of mercy may seem curious, especially because the close connections between Luke and Acts show that the apostles continued the ministry of Jesus. Acts narrates the story of the apostles, especially Peter and Paul, as they fulfill the commands of Jesus told in Luke. Scholars point to innumerable verbal connections between the two books. Many of the themes announced in Luke continue in Acts. Yet, this is not the case with the theme of mercy, at least regarding the vocabulary.

There is, however, more continuity between "Luke, the Gospel of Mercy" and Acts than meets the eye. Acts may not explicitly employ the vocabulary of mercy in its stories of the apostles' ministry, but mercy is *implicit* throughout. The following five episodes in the growth of the nascent Church illustrate this fact.

- Just after Pentecost (Acts 2), one finds the story of the crippled beggar who asks for alms from two apostles, Peter and John. Peter responds that he has no money to give, but he offers him something far greater—a cure "in the name of Jesus Christ of Nazareth" (3:1–10).
- After Paul's conversion, Peter goes down to Lydda and heals the paralyzed man named Aeneas (9:32–35; note that Peter says, "Jesus Christ heals you").
- There follows the episode of Peter raising Tabitha from the dead (9:36–41).
- On one of his missionary ventures, Paul restores the young man Eutychus to life after he falls out a window and dies (20:7–12).

- Near the end of Acts, Paul's ministry of boldly preaching the gospel message continues, and he quotes the long passage that speaks of the hardness of Israel's heart yet holds out the hope for healing (28:26–27; cf. Isa 6:9–10), in effect, hinting at the merciful action of God.

What do these five episodes suggest? Even if they do not employ the language of mercy, they *show* that the mercy already evident in the ministry of Jesus described by Luke's Gospel is equally present in the ministry of the apostles after Pentecost. In other words, these stories describe *mercy in action,* not mere words.

It is equally significant that the apostles perform many of the same kinds of miracles and healings that Jesus did, including raising the dead. In other words, they continue to implement Jesus' ministerial vision. Acts summarizes this apostolic ministry with these words: "Many signs and wonders were done among the people through the apostles" (5:12). Therefore, in its own way, Acts reinforces the message of mercy begun in the ministry of Jesus and then announced formally at the synagogue in Nazareth, using the words of the Prophet Isaiah (Luke 4:16–21; Isa 61:1–2; 58:6).

REFLECTION QUESTIONS

1. Why is Luke considered the "Gospel of mercy"? Do you find this designation accurate?
2. Can you identify two examples in Luke's Gospel where Jesus is particularly portrayed as compassionate and merciful?
3. How do you reconcile Luke's portrayal of Jesus as merciful with his seemingly harsh reaction to the buying and selling in the Jerusalem temple (19:45–

48)? Should not Jesus be merciful to the merchants, too?

4. Many identify the parable of the prodigal son (Luke 15:11–32) as the quintessential example of mercy in Luke. What if you were the older son? How would you feel? How does his perspective fit into the story of the merciful father?
5. Why is mercy not explicitly mentioned in the Acts of the Apostles? Is the Church not called upon to be merciful?

CHAPTER 5

SAINT PAUL AND THE MERCY OF GOD

But for that very reason I [Paul] received mercy, so that in me, as the foremost, Jesus Christ might display the utmost patience, making me an example to those who would come to believe in him for eternal life. (1 Tim 1:16)

When the average person in the pew thinks of Saint Paul, they likely do not connect him with the theme of mercy. Many people have the mistaken idea that Paul was judgmental and not very merciful. They think that he was not particularly accepting of women, that he preached against homosexuals, and that he was generally impulsive and intolerant. Such misconceptions deserve a closer look. Although we will defer some especially difficult topics to the next chapter, we will begin, in this chapter, with a general orientation to mercy in the Pauline letters.

PAUL'S PERSONAL EXPERIENCE OF MERCY

With Paul, the place to begin is his own "conversion" experience. The Acts of the Apostles recounts the famous story of Paul's dramatic conversion on the road to Damascus, while he is searching to arrest followers of "the Way," the early Christian designation for Christianity (see Acts 9:1–9). A light suddenly flashes about him, and he falls to the ground, hearing a voice saying, "Saul, Saul, why do you persecute me?" The voice says he will be told what to do, but when he arises, he is blind and must be led by the hand to the house of Ananias. Eventually, of course, Paul learns that God intends him to be the missionary to the Gentiles; he is baptized, and his remarkable ministry begins.

As powerful as this story is, it is not the way Paul describes it. Paul uses the language of "revelation" (Gal 1:12 and 16) to describe what essentially is not a conversion in the classic sense—that is, a change of religion—but a prophetic call or commissioning. Paul's self-description of the event in Galatians is worth recalling:

> But when God, who had set me apart before I was born and called me through his grace, was pleased to reveal his Son to me, so that I might proclaim him among the Gentiles.... (1:15–16)

The language is similar to other prophetic calls (e.g., Isaiah [Isa 49:1] and Jeremiah [Jer 4:1]). From his mother's womb, Paul was destined to be the missionary to the Gentiles. He views this entirely as God's gracious action toward him. God's grace reached out and touched him, transforming him from ardent persecutor to foremost proclaimer of the gospel message. He also sees it as God's love. As he describes it in Galatians: "And the life I now live in the flesh I live by faith in the Son of God, who loved me and gave himself for me" (2:20). This is one of those instances where Paul's language is almost emotional. The personal love he experienced in his transformation was nothing less than the mercy of God at work in his life through the cross of Christ. He is a foremost recipient of God's loving mercy, despite his having persecuted the Church. He holds nothing back in praising God for the mercy he has received in Christ.

Elsewhere, in Second Corinthians, Paul makes the explicit connection between his ministry (and that of his companions) and God's mercy. He writes in defense of their common apostolic ministry: "Therefore, *since it is by God's mercy* that we are engaged in this ministry, we do not lose heart" (2 Cor 4:1).[1] The context of this passage concerns the persecution and hardships the apostles often endured. But the main point is that God's mercy is what brought them to this ministry, and that same mercy sustains them in it.

Another passage is even more explicit when Paul writes to Timothy. Admitting his history of persecution and violence, Paul says he nonetheless "received mercy (Gk. *ēleēthēn*) because I had acted ignorantly in unbelief" (1 Tim 1:13). Just a few lines later, Paul refers to the importance that this reception of mercy means for others:

> But for that very reason I received mercy, so that in me, as the foremost, Jesus Christ might display the utmost patience, making me an example to those who would come to believe in him for eternal life. (1:16)

We see here also the close connection between God's mercy and patience. Being a personal recipient of God's mercy, despite his checkered background, has made Paul an example for others. If *he* can receive God's mercy, then *anyone* can.

In fact, elsewhere, Paul indicates that he was not the only recipient of God's mercy. In Philippians, he recounts the story of his colleague Epaphroditus, a figure well known in Philippi and a companion of Paul in ministry. At one point, Epaphroditus falls seriously ill, which is partly why Paul writes the Letter to the Philippians, to prepare them for Epaphroditus's premature return. Paul explains,

> He was indeed so ill that he nearly died. But God had mercy (Gk. *ēleēsen*) on him, and not only on him but on me also, so that I would not have one sorrow after another. (Phil 2:27)

God's mercy that Paul describes here is twofold. It falls upon Epaphroditus, who is cured of his illness, and it also affects Paul, who does not have to experience the tragic loss of a beloved companion. It's as if mercy had a ripple effect, from one to the other. God's mercy touched both.

In short, the foundation of Paul's understanding of God's mercy can be found in his own experience of having received God's mercy personally. He (and his colleagues) have been recipients of God's mercy (e.g., 2 Cor 4:1), and he appeals to others through "the mercies (Gk. *oiktirmōn*; plural) of God" (Rom 12:1). But his understanding goes beyond his mere personal experience.

THE GOD OF MERCY

Paul's letters demonstrate in multiple ways that he understands mercy to be one of the characteristics of God's very identity, a teaching we have seen throughout this book, and which is characteristic of the Jewish perspective of the Old Testament. This is evident here in three primary ways.

The first way is in the greeting or thanksgiving sections of his letters. For instance, in the thanksgiving prayer of Second Corinthians, Paul writes,

> Blessed be the God and Father of our Lord Jesus Christ, the Father of mercies and the God of all consolation, who consoles us in all our affliction, so that we may be able to console those who are in any affliction with the consolation with which we ourselves are consoled by God. (1:3–4)

Here, Paul shows his deep understanding that God is a "Father of mercies" and a "God of all consolation." Mercy and consolation in times of affliction are affirmed as characteristic of God's identity. In fact, notice that Paul employs the same root for "consolation/console" no fewer than five times in two verses. This prayer forms an introduction to what Paul will discuss later in this letter, namely his understanding of ministry and the hardships it entails (e.g., 2 Cor 4:7–11; 6:1–10). In the context of such a difficult and challenging ministry, which often brings with it attendant suffering and affliction, knowing that God is merciful and consoling provides important encouragement to persevere. Therefore, Paul continues to move forward in proclaiming the gospel message. He trusts in God's consolation and mercy. Elsewhere he acknowledges that it was God's mercy alone that allowed for his salvation, not any righteous deeds on his part (Titus 3:5). He also affirms that God is "rich in mercy," implying a superabundance of the virtue (Eph 2:4).

A second way in which Paul shows his understanding of God's mercy is through his argumentation. The best example is the extended attempt in Romans 9—11 to explain how God will ultimately bring about salvation for the Jews, Paul's own people, despite their consistent resistance to accept Jesus as God's Son and the Messiah. While we cannot do justice here to this impressive passage, we can nevertheless glance at how Paul employs the theme of mercy. He uses the Greek verb *eleeō* ("have mercy") eight times in these chapters, and the noun *eleos* ("mercy") three times. So, it is fair to say that mercy is one of the overarching themes of the passage. The argumentation of these three chapters of Romans is notoriously complex.

(I will admit, Paul is often not easily understood or interpreted, but his profound message warrants the work involved.) One sees Paul struggling to explain what is ultimately mystery. He is sorely troubled that the Gentiles have paradoxically accepted the gospel message more readily than his own people. How will Israel be saved if they do not accept the Messiah? What will happen to the people of the original covenant?

Paul begins by recalling for his mostly Gentile readers/hearers God's plan, citing numerous passages from the Old Testament and emphasizing that the Jews are children of God's "promise." He explicitly cites a passage from Exodus where God speaks to Moses:

> For he [God] says to Moses, / "I will have mercy on whom I have mercy, / and I will have compassion on whom I have compassion." (Rom 9:15; Exod 33:19)

He is invoking the Old Testament image of a merciful God, such as we explored in chapter 2. Paul's conclusion is simple, as expressed in the next verse: "So it depends not on human will or exertion, but on God who shows mercy" (Rom 9:16). This puts God in the driver's seat, we might say. God can choose to distribute his mercy and his compassion as God chooses. God's mercy is indiscriminate. It is dependent neither on our worthiness (or lack thereof) nor on our deeds.

As his argument progresses, Paul not only reiterates a basic principle he accepts—that God shows no partiality, either to Jew or Gentile (Rom 10:12)—but also that God has not rejected his chosen people Israel (11:1). Instead, Paul explains, the reversal of fortune experienced by the Gentiles through God's mercy will also come upon Israel. The Gentiles' faith will ironically create a jealous reaction, whereby Israel will desire to come to faith and thus be saved. As he nears the conclusion of his argument, Paul spells out his understanding:

> Just as you were once disobedient to God but have now received mercy because of their disobedience, so they have now been disobedient in order that, by the mercy shown to you, they too may now receive mercy. (11:30–31)

What a twist of fate! What an act of mercy! Paul basically says that salvation history has witnessed a remarkable and gracious act of mercy, not once but twice. God has found a path to ensure that *all* can be saved, whether Gentile or Jew.

Paul caps his argument with this strong assertion: "For God delivered all to disobedience, that he might have mercy upon all" (Rom 11:32 NABRE). If the Gentiles were once distant from God, God's mercy ultimately reached out through Jesus Christ to bring them into the fold. This gracious action will likewise have a positive effect on Israel, who will, in the end, receive God's mercy. Near the end of Romans, Paul reinforces this message by repeating his understanding that God will be faithful to the promises made to Israel but at the same time will welcome the Gentiles into the family of faith (15:8–9). All this is due to God's mercy, which knows no bounds.

The argumentation is complex, to be sure. But Paul's conviction shines through: the God of mercy and compassion will not disappoint. Somehow—and Paul is not quite sure how to explain it, for it is mystery—God's mercy will embrace *all*, even Israel.

RECONCILIATION: MERCY IN ACTION

A third example of Paul's deep understanding of God's mercy is found especially in Second Corinthians on the theme of reconciliation. The passage in question (2 Cor 5:16–21) is the New Testament's most extensive treatment of the concept of reconciliation, which for Roman Catholics especially, is focused on the sacrament of the same name. Three key ideas emerge from this passage, and all three give us a glimpse of Paul's profound understanding that in Jesus Christ, God has acted most mercifully and graciously toward the human race.

The first idea is the notion of "new creation" that comes from life in Christ: "So if anyone is in Christ, there is a new creation: everything old has passed away; see, everything has become new!" (5:17). Entry into the life of Christ, by baptism, brings about a totally new existence, according to Paul. The old no longer exists; we have a new chance, a new beginning, a new opportunity to live in accord with God's will. This is good news indeed, for we know that sinfulness abounds in contemporary human circumstances, yet this reality need not be permanent. Paul sees a totally "new creation" at work in Christ; human divisions as well as our separation from God by our sinfulness are not the last word. From this angle, we can understand the teaching of Paul about the unity that is found in Christ.

> There is no longer Jew or Greek, there is no longer slave or free, there is no longer male and female; for all of you are one in Christ Jesus. (Gal 3:28; see also Rom 10:12; 1 Cor 12:13; Col 3:11)

The second aspect is Paul's affirmation of the divine origin of this reconciliation: "All this is from God, who reconciled us to himself through Christ...that is, in Christ God was reconciling the world to himself, not counting their trespasses against them" (2 Cor 5:18–19). God is clearly the source of this reconciliation. It is God's mercy in action. God does not hold our sinfulness against us. Instead, God has shown us a great mercy by sending his Son, the Christ, to "reconcile" the world to himself.

Finally, one sees in this divine action a call to human participation. Twice, Paul reminds the Corinthians of their role in carrying this divine mercy forward by repeating the phrase of entrusting to us the ministry of reconciliation (vv. 18–19). Paul even uses the title of "ambassador" for those who are entrusted with this ministry of reconciliation. An ambassador is one who has authority to speak and act for the one he represents, in this case, Christ himself. So, the ministry of reconciliation, which is entrusted to the faith community, is nothing less than a participation in Christ's own ministry of reconciliation. As we have received mercy and have been reconciled to God, so we are asked to extend that same mercy to others.

So, Paul explicitly sees reconciliation as an effect of the Christ-event and as an essential aspect of his own ministry and indeed of the entire Church. Extending mercy promotes reconciliation, and the result can only be a better world. All believers should be willing to show mercy to others through their deeply felt compassion (Col 3:12).[2]

A FURTHER QUESTION

So far, this exposé of Paul's understanding of mercy is likely appealing. Paul is one of the most surprising and nuanced sources of New Testament teaching on God's mercy. But a problem arises for many people when they think of Paul the Apostle. Their consternation is centered on the perception that Paul may have spoken well about mercy in words, but his actions toward some people, women and homosexuals, specifically, show otherwise. They sometimes ask, "Was he, at heart, a prejudiced individual who only showed mercy to those of whom he approved but not to others?" This topic opens the proverbial can of worms that we will treat in a separate chapter, to which we now turn.

REFLECTION QUESTIONS

1. How do you respond to the suggestion that Saint Paul was also a merciful person? Does this match your own perceptions of Paul?
2. In what way(s) does Paul say he has been a recipient of God's mercy? Does receiving God's mercy place any obligation upon those who receive it?
3. How would you relate mercy to Paul's primary ethical teaching of the three most important virtues: faith, hope, and love?
4. Why should Paul's conversion be considered a call or a commission? How does this experience relate to his approach to mercy?
5. How would you explain Paul's teaching that God's mercy is evident in the experience of reconciliation? How do you understand the concept of reconciliation?

CHAPTER 6

SAINT PAUL REVISITED: MISPERCEPTIONS ABOUT MERCY?

> *Just as you were once disobedient to God but have now received mercy because of their disobedience, so they have now been disobedient in order that, by the mercy shown to you, they too may now receive mercy.* (Rom 11:30–31)

In the previous chapter, we examined the general perspective of the mercy of God in Paul's letters. I suggested that Paul has a rather surprising view of mercy, especially compared to the way he is usually perceived by many Christians. I also noted, however, that there are some delicate passages in Paul's letters, especially concerning "hot button" topics like the roles of women or homosexuality, that could benefit from a separate study. That is the purpose of this chapter.

MISPERCEIVING PAUL

The impetus for my concern is a lingering attitude in the popular mind that Paul had almost irredeemably negative attitudes toward women and homosexual persons. Others imply he was obsessed with sex or perhaps was sexually repressed. From an objective biblical perspective, I view such judgments as anachronistic and lacking nuance. Moreover, I think there is an underlying crypto-fundamentalist attitude that wants to see every modern trend or tendency justified somehow in the Bible. It seems to be a way to rationalize our own modern preoccupations. Our modern cultural context, especially in the West, is obsessed with issues of sexuality in a way that goes far beyond any New Testament document, let alone Paul's letters. The fact is that there are only a few passages that address such topics. So we should not exaggerate Paul's teachings on such delicate themes because of our modern biases.

PAUL AND SEXUALITY

The starting point to understand Paul's views on gender and sex is both his culture and his religious tenets, which are thoroughly Jewish. Paul, like Jesus of Nazareth or any of the apostles, was a man of his time. When Paul addressed questions about sexuality, it was often because his communities asked him for advice in such cases. Take, for example, the second half of First Corinthians. Paul begins, "Now concerning the matters *about which you wrote*..." (1 Cor 7:1). Paul writes because the Corinthians have asked his opinion about some difficult situations. He is thus responding in a pastoral context.

In the dual Jewish and Greco-Roman worlds in which Paul operated, there were stereotypical roles for men and women, for masters and slaves, for children and adults. Paul had no way to escape these influences, though it is clear in his letters that the Christian faith to which he came by God's grace dramatically impacted his views of social relationships. (We will come to that shortly.)

In the Greco-Roman world, women had more freedom than in the traditional Jewish household of Palestine. Paul, a Jew born in the Diaspora, would have been familiar with both viewpoints. His own views on sexuality, which are not expressed at great length in his letters, come from his Jewish upbringing. Like Jesus, Paul went back to Genesis and the origins of God creating man and woman in God's own likeness. Both genders reflect the divine being.

Moreover, far from being prudish about sexuality, Paul understood genital sexual relations as part and parcel of marriage between a man and a woman. A man with hang-ups on sex would hardly admit, in his longest treatment of sex and marriage, that a married couple should "not deprive one another," except in instances of prayerful asceticism for a time (1 Cor 7:5). Like any good rabbi who sees value in sexual abstinence for spiritual reasons, he nonetheless asserts, "If they [the unmarried] are not practicing self-control, they should marry. For it is better to marry than to be aflame with passion" (7:9). These are not the words of someone who is sexually repressed. This is simple rabbinic advice that fulfills God's command in Genesis to the man and woman to "be fruitful and multiply" (Gen 1:28). At the same time, because certain situations had arisen in Corinth concerning incest and divorce, Paul offers his advice based upon his understanding of Scripture as God's law, but also within his own context. Note that two influences underlie the context of First Corinthians. One is the strong tone of apocalyptic expectation, in which Paul urges all to remain as they are (single or married) because "the present form of this world is passing away" (7:31). The other influence is Paul's insistence that God desires their happiness. God does not want them to be "anxious" (7:32–35). Worrying over such matters will only create anxieties. That is why Paul urges them to stay as they are and not "rock the boat."

In short, Paul's overarching views on gender and sexuality are consistent with his Jewish ancestry. And because they are rooted in the biblical (Old Testament) teaching, he sees God's message as promoting happiness among people, not dissatisfaction.

To the burning question of other forms of marriage (e.g., homosexual marriage), Paul would not even be able to envision such a reality. While we will treat the question of homosexuality below, here we can only admit that such a modern scenario rooted in secular Western culture goes beyond anything the Bible could envision. This does not mean contemporary Christians have *nothing* to say on the topic. Nor does it mean that we cannot glean some basic principles from the Bible to address such issues. It simply admits that one cannot find justification in the Bible for such a relationship. For Paul, *marriage* could only mean the covenant relationship between a man and a woman established by God at Creation.

THE CASE OF WOMEN

But what about women? For modern ears, the most problematic Pauline passages are those that seemingly restrict the roles of women in the Church or in the family.

Two responses are needed to this question. The first is to admit that there are Pauline passages that seemingly restrict certain liturgical roles, such as insisting that women "be silent in the churches" (1 Cor 14:33b–36). These verses may be an interpolation from a later time, and consequently may not reflect Paul's own view. Yet they are found in the New Testament, so we cannot simply dismiss them. More important is to recognize that elsewhere Paul clearly acknowledges that women *can* "prophesy" (11:4–5). Although these verses address the issue of time-conditioned customs concerning head coverings appropriate to males or females in that time, notice nonetheless that the passage presumes both men *and* women can prophesy. If that is the case, then surely women as well as men can speak in the Church. Additionally, we should recall that nearly half the names of Paul's colleagues in ministry are women. Some are married couples that functioned as "teams" (like Prisca and Aquila; Rom 16:3), and others are individuals. Clearly, Paul did not bar women from ministry. Phoebe, from the house church in Cenchreae, is even called a "deacon" (Rom 16:1, Gk. *diakonos*), clearly evoking some formal ministerial role in the Church. The fact that the Greek word *deacon* is in the masculine form and not the feminine further implies some form of official ministry, although it is difficult to determine precisely what the exact duties of a deacon in those days were.

Another difficult passage is the famous comparison in Ephesians of the union of husband and wife with that of Christ and the Church. Again, scholars think it may have developed after Paul and thus does not reflect Paul's own views. Nonetheless, the passage is in the Bible and, indeed, is read at liturgy. What should we say about wives being subject to their husbands?

This is a complex passage. It is not a justification for consigning women to the kitchen! What is usually glossed over is that its whole context is based upon *mutual* obedience, not the husband lording it over the wife. The beginning of the chapter calls for imitating God by living in love (Eph 5:1). Then, when the image of marriage is reached, the first line is, "Be subject (Gk. *hypotassō*) to one another" (5:21), using the same verb as the wife being subordinate to the husband (Eph 5:24). Notice that the Greek verb meaning "be subordinate" or "subject to" implies obedience from a lesser to a greater authority. Yet Paul uses it in the context of *mutual* submission before applying it to the more restrictive role. Even more important is that Ephesians calls on husbands to "love" their wives as their very selves. In other words, the husband's duty is to have the same kind of love that Christ has for the Church. This is hardly soft on the position of the husband. Love, for Paul, is the highest virtue, and he knows well that it can be difficult to live in the flesh. So the passage is not nearly so restrictive of the wife's role in marriage as some would make it out to be.

One more piece of Pauline perspective should be added here. Although Paul had some views of men and women's roles as dictated by his culture, we glimpse an alternative kind of existence rooted in his Christian faith. The prime passage is this:

> There is no longer Jew or Greek, there is no longer slave or free, there is no longer male and female; for all of you are one in Christ Jesus. (Gal 3:28)

Paul knew that once one was joined to Christ by baptism, relationships changed. All became brothers and sisters in the Lord. This may have been a Pauline ideal hard to live out concretely, but it indicates that Paul could grow beyond the limitations of his upbringing.

DID PAUL HATE HOMOSEXUALS?

On the question of homosexuality, Paul was also a man of his time, culture, and religion. Compared to the surrounding Greco-Roman culture, Judaism was more restrictive on the question of homosexuality.[1] Those who want to interpret the Bible in ways that rationalize contemporary preferences or behavior are bound to be disappointed. As a first-century Jew, Paul simply viewed homosexual activity as sinful and a corruption of what God intended. As with his Jewish contemporaries, homosexual behavior was particularly associated with the Greco-Roman world. Jews generally considered it an aberration. This is the context for his teaching on homosexuality, which, in fact, is restricted to just a few passages. Paul was hardly obsessed with the question.

In Romans 1—3, the context of a "theological" analysis of what is wrong in the world—embracing both Gentiles and Jews—explains why *all* need a Savior. Paul sees genital homosexual activity as part of the idolatrous situation of the Greco-Roman world, in which people have forgotten the Creator and have become disoriented and seduced by self-indulgence. Paul sees this homosexual activity, whether male or female, as symptomatic of the larger failure of the Greco-Roman world: idolatry. He goes on in Romans 2 to be equally harsh about his own Jewish context, where, with the Torah, one should have known better. But note well: there is no blanket condemnation of homosexuality. Paul knew nothing of sexual orientation. That is a modern concept. He could not distinguish identity or orientation from actions. The actions are what Paul views as sinful. But the situation is not irredeemable. On the contrary, all who are sinners, that is, all human beings, need the saving action of Jesus Christ.

One could make similar comments about two other passages in Paul's letters where the context is equally compelling (1 Cor 6:9–10; 1 Tim 1:10). Homosexual genital activity, and particularly cavorting with young male prostitutes, which did occur in the Greco-Roman world, Paul views as a perversion of God's law. Note that in First Corinthians, Paul even says,

> And this is what some of you used to be. But you were washed, you were sanctified, you were justified in the name of the Lord Jesus Christ and in the Spirit of our God. (6:11)

Their past is not their future. Their previous sinful acts have not condemned them. Their acceptance of the free salvation offered by God in Jesus Christ has cleansed them and reoriented them toward their ultimate goal of union with God in the kingdom.

WHAT DOES MERCY HAVE TO DO WITH IT?

What I have attempted to show in an all-too-limited way is that it is not fair to condemn Paul for alleged misogyny or promoting mistreatment of women or people of homosexual orientation. These are complex contemporary issues. They were far less prominent in Paul's day. Yet he remained, and remains, a man of his era. Despite his profound understanding of the message of Jesus Christ, he could not see, for instance, the limitations of certain cultural aspects of his time. Men and women had distinct and restrictive roles. Slavery was simply a given in the background, although Paul clearly thought Christians were equal "brothers and sisters" (e.g., see Phlm 16). Homosexuality was a characteristic of secular Greco-Roman life that Jews especially found distasteful. In none of these instances does Paul provide a blanket condemnation of persons.[2]

Oscar Wilde reportedly said, "Every saint has a past, and every sinner has a future." This is an admission that no one in this life is perfect. It also opines that no one's present situation, regardless of how sinful or depraved it may seem to be, is irredeemable. There is no room in the teaching of Jesus for casting stones against those who don't yet measure up to the ideal standards of the kingdom of heaven to which all are called.

In practical terms, those of us engaged in ministry should be careful not to condemn the sinner; yet we likewise cannot condone sinful actions. The two are, perhaps, hard to distinguish. It is a difficult path to maneuver. But this is precisely what Pope Francis called the Church to do during the Year of Mercy, and at its end, he invited people to continue the same path. What mercy has to do with it is *everything*. We might say, the Church is of necessity in the business of mercy. As the community of faith, we have an obligation to proclaim authentically the good news that we have received from the biblical tradition and that the Church preserves in its own preaching and teaching. The Church's message of mercy is intended not to condemn or shame people but to call them to spiritual transformation. Saint Paul would wholeheartedly concur.

Saint Paul, by any measure, was a onetime, law-observant Pharisee whose transformation by God's grace into *the* Apostle to the Gentiles molded him into a formidable and zealous evangelizer. Yes, he called his communities to a more righteous way of life. (So did Jesus [Matt 5:20].) Yes, he sometimes berated them for their failure to stay on the right path. Yes, he occasionally expressed his utter perplexity and frustration with the lack of progress in some of the communities, as with his stubborn Galatians (Gal 4:20). But he never let that stop him from proclaiming the good news of Jesus Christ. His overarching vision was not one of setting up boundaries and walls but of calling his communities to a better way of life together. His ministry was not to condemn but to transform. If he had cultural limits based upon his era and restricted experience, which do not always translate well in a one-to-one correspondence in our time, he nonetheless taught that the mercy of God could overcome every obstacle.

REFLECTION QUESTIONS

1. Why do you think Saint Paul has been so misunderstood and maligned throughout Christian history? Is this fair to his legacy?
2. Do you think Saint Paul harbored negative opinions about women and about homosexuals? In what way(s) should these perceptions be nuanced?
3. What is the relationship between being merciful to someone and yet not necessarily affirming their life choices? Is it possible to separate the sin from the sinner? That is, can you condemn the sin but not the person who commits the sin?

4. What do you make of Saint Paul's ethical teachings in the context of proclaiming God's mercy? What role does ethics play in Paul's thought?
5. How do you understand the role of women in Paul's faith communities? Why is it inaccurate to say that Paul did not tolerate women in ministry?

CHAPTER 7

MERCY IN THE CHURCH AND IN THE MODERN WORLD

Blessed are the merciful, for they will receive mercy. (Matt 5:7)

One of the great hallmarks of the Second Vatican Council (1962–65), whose fiftieth anniversary led to a flood of publications on the impact of the council, was the Church's evident attempt to relate to the modern world. Pope (now Saint) John XXIII had always intended a pastoral council, one whose outreach to the modern world would be most evident. He intentionally called for the council not to look merely inward but outward, to reinvigorate its evangelization efforts but also to do a better job at communicating the Church's message of the gospel of Jesus Christ.

No conciliar text makes this clearer than the Pastoral Constitution on the Church in the Modern World (*Gaudium et Spes*, 1965), whose opening lines are the following:

> The joys and the hopes, the griefs and the anxieties of the [people] of this age, especially those who are poor or in any way afflicted, these are the joys and hopes, the griefs and anxieties of the followers of Christ. Indeed, nothing genuinely human fails to raise an echo in their hearts. (§1)

The council fathers go on to explain their rationale: "For the council yearns to explain to everyone how it conceives of the presence and activity of the Church in the world of today" (§2).

There are, of course, those who will immediately raise a cry of alarm that the Church is interfering in politics. "Mind your own business," they will say, "and let us mind ours." It is true that the Church should scrupulously avoid partisan behavior. It can lead to serious division and create factionalism. Nonetheless, when ethical concerns arise, either on the level of individuals or nations, the Church not only has the right but the obligation to speak, just as the prophets of the Old Testament did. Therefore, recent Church teachings have indeed broached many modern ethical topics, including some of the most controversial ones like abortion, the death penalty, medical ethics, human trafficking, care of refugees, racism, the nuclear arms race, and a multitude of other issues.

We cannot bury our heads in the sand and pretend that such problems do not confront virtually all humanity. The world has become ever smaller because of advances in travel, technology, and communications. As Pope Francis warned in his 2015 encyclical letter on ecological issues confronting the world, *Laudato Si'* ("Praise be to You"),[1] we all have a common home, called Earth. Because we are all on this planet together, we all bear some responsibility for its care. God made all humanity stewards of this our common home, and this means all share some ethical responsibility. The Church is not exempted from this obligation.

This situation is also why recent popes, from Pope Saint John XXIII to Pope Francis, have spoken out on modern ethical issues and have also drawn serious attention to the theme of mercy that, in accord with Church teaching and gospel ethics, should be applied to many situations in our day. In a world where there is increasing fear and anxiety, where refugees fleeing violence and extreme poverty are seeking safe havens in vast numbers, and where many nations have tried to build walls or to raise the bridges, we might say, to bolster one's own protection, the message of mercy is sorely needed.

To pull together the threads of our discussion throughout this book, we will summarize some main teachings in two categories. The first will be a summary of the Bible's own teaching of mercy in the way I have tried to explain it here. The second will summarize some recent Church teachings about mercy that attempt to implement the vision enunciated at Vatican Council II.

A SUMMARY OF THE BIBLICAL PERSPECTIVE ON MERCY

Without desiring to repeat the information in the previous six chapters, I propose the following series of concise statements about the biblical teaching on mercy, embracing both Old and New Testaments.

First, *the Bible's teaching about mercy is complex*. It cannot be reduced to one assertion. It is as broad as it is deep. In part, this is because the Bible consists of a library of books that came into existence through oral and written traditions spanning many centuries. God's inspired Word, of necessity, applied to different circumstances in different periods according to what was needed. Inevitably, this led to different emphases in different books.

Second, *the Bible's vocabulary of mercy is also broad and deep*. It expresses attitudes, feelings, and most importantly, saving actions. It includes the concepts of mercy, graciousness, kindness, pity, compassion, empathy, steadfast faithfulness, favor, and love. Mercy innately comes from the depths of one's being. It is seen in the ability to enter into another's suffering and pain and to offer saving, life-giving help.

Third, there is *no justification for the tenacious caricature of the God of the Old Testament as vengeful and the God of the New Testament as loving and merciful.* It is amazing how often this false impression continues to arise, but it does. The God of the Old Testament and the Father of Jesus Christ are one and the same; Jesus himself mirrors his Father's mercy.

Fourth, in close relationship to the previous point, *the Bible's teaching on mercy is unified.* That is, despite some diversity of language and imagery, there is one consistent thread of mercy running through both Testaments; there is no division between the Old and New Testaments. Even though circumstances and emphases might be different, God's merciful nature shines throughout the Bible.

Fifth, *mercy is the quintessential aspect of God.* God can be none other than merciful. It is the quality that shows the uniqueness of the God of Abraham, Isaac, and Jacob, the God of Israel. It is in God's very nature to be merciful, even if at times, the threatened punishment against a stubborn and rebellious people must be carried out as an occasion for just recompense for evil deeds.

Sixth, intimately tied to God's merciful nature is *the tendency to infinite patience,* even when we human beings, time and again, stray from God's own commandments.

Seventh, *mercy is an essential characteristic of the teaching of Jesus of Nazareth.* Jesus was (and is) indeed the "face of the Father's mercy." Even if one wanted (improperly, as we saw) to say that the Old Testament is not uniformly a text about mercy, one cannot escape the fact that Jesus' essential message revolved around mercy, forgiveness, and love. He radicalized the teaching of love and mercy in the Old Testament, making it the heart of the Christian message.

Eighth, *God demands of humanity the same quality of mercy that is characteristic of the divine identity.* We human beings are to be merciful like God. Or, to quote the motto of the Year of Mercy, we are to be "merciful like the Father."

Ninth, *mercy is not merely an option but an obligation*. It is a characteristic of the kingdom of God toward which we are to strive without ceasing. This understanding likely developed over time in the biblical history, but in the end, both the Jewish people and Christians came to believe that mercy was a divine quality that humans were expected to acquire.

Tenth, *mercy is not merely "cheap grace,"* to use the expression of Dietrich Bonhoeffer, the Lutheran pastor martyred by the Nazis during World War II. Mercy in the Bible also does not mean ignoring the consequences of sin and evil. Mercy does not overlook injustice but attempts to reconcile it, to transform it, to heal it. Mercy and justice, in fact, often go together, but the Bible also makes it clear that mercy ultimately trumps justice, just as love trumps sternness. Thus, as the Psalmist says, "Mercy and faithfulness will meet; justice and peace shall kiss" (Ps 85:10, au. trans.).

Eleventh, *mercy is closely related to other deeply human sentiments, of which love is the most important*. One thinks of concepts like tenderness, charity, leniency, clemency, or compassion. Each of these expresses a nuance, but they are interrelated concepts. In fact, mercy and compassion are simply aspects of love, and love is the first and absolute command of Jesus Christ. When asked about the greatest commandment, Jesus responds,

> "You shall love the Lord your God with all your heart, and with all your soul, and with all your mind." This is the greatest and first commandment. And a second is like it: "You shall love your neighbor as yourself." On these two commandments hang all the law and the prophets. (Matt 22:37–40)

Love of God and love of neighbor go hand in hand. You cannot have one without the other (see also James 2:18–22).

Twelfth, *mercy and forgiveness also go together*. Being merciful means being able to forgive, even, as Jesus says, "seventy-seven times" (Matt 18:22; an image for limitless forgiveness). Mercy leads to reconciliation between God and humanity and even among human beings. Being forgiven ideally leads one to extend forgiveness to others (see Matt 18:21–35).

Thirteenth, *mercy is always relational*. It is a social reality. It has personal, communal, and even international dimensions, touching relationships among individuals, communities, and nations. Ideally, mercy is operative in the lives of individuals and in the conduct of nations to avoid conflict, hatred, violence, and war. Sadly, many have wrongly used religion to promote the opposite of mercy, willfully committing barbarous acts in the name of religion or divine justice. This is the opposite of mercy; it does not constitute divine justice.

Fourteenth, for most of us, *mercy is not easy to put into practice*, in particular, if it means being willing to forgive someone who has truly offended us or perhaps even done us great harm. The human thirst for vengeance is, sadly, very strong. This is one reason why mercy cannot merely be a partial theme or a onetime occurrence in our lives. It is meant to be a way of life, especially for us who follow Jesus.

Fifteenth, *the biblical teaching on mercy is the foundation for the Church's teaching on mercy*. The Church's message is not new. Rather, it is an attempt to repeat and apply in new circumstances the age-old biblical message of mercy.

These fifteen statements provide a basic summary of the Bible's teaching on mercy. They do not show explicitly the disparate number of images the Bible uses to describe God's mercy, such as in the prophetic literature or the parables of Jesus. But they do show the breadth of the biblical teaching across both Testaments. The message is inescapable: mercy is a major teaching of the Bible, from Genesis to Revelation.

AN ECCLESIAL PERSPECTIVE ON MERCY

Building upon the information just discussed concerning mercy in the Bible, the Church has tried, especially in the years since Vatican II, to bring this perspective to bear on the real, pastoral situations that exist in the modern world. Without any pretense at completeness, I again suggest some basic directions that emerge from the Church's teaching on mercy, especially as expressed by Pope Francis and his immediate predecessors.

POPE FRANCIS: A CONCRETE EXAMPLE

One can find a concrete example of the delicate balance between justice and mercy in an action of Pope Francis. In February 2017, it was revealed that the pope had written a preface to an Italian book titled *La Perdono, Padre* (*They Forgive You, Father*).[2] The author, Daniel Pittet, is a Swiss victim of sexual abuse as a minor at the hands of a priest. The abuse lasted four years, and the psychological scars were, and are, very deep. But he wrote the book ultimately to express his forgiveness of the perpetrator—after many years of therapy and struggles, to be sure—which gives the book its title.

It is rare for popes to engage in promotion of published writings, except their own perhaps. But Pope Francis felt strongly enough to do it. He had, in fact, met Mr. Pittet at the Vatican in 2015 and was impressed with his story. In the preface to the book, the pope expresses the scandal and the horror of sexual abuse of minors by clergy. He also minces no words about bishops who may have protected priest perpetrators. "How can a priest in the service of Christ and his Church cause so much evil?" the pope writes, adding, "This is an absolute monstrosity, a horrendous sin, completely opposed to what Christ teaches us." He goes on to ask forgiveness from the victims and their families.

My point in citing this example is that what ultimately brings some form of peace and tranquility to such a heart-wrenching situation is the mercy of God and the ability to tap into it. Human mercy does not come cheap. It is not automatic, and perhaps it even runs counter to our human tendency to seek revenge, to want to make someone else suffer as much, if not more, than they made us suffer. Yet it seems that only the ability to work through the pain and arrive at a point where one can forgive even terrible perpetrators of evil grants victims some form of internal peace. That does not mean that all the emotional scars will suddenly disappear. Nor does it mean that deep-seated hurt and vengeful desires will not, on occasion, bubble to the surface and disturb the desired tranquility. What is clear, though, is that only arriving at a point where one can indeed extend mercy and forgiveness can help soothe the hurt that comes with being so violently violated. The pope's preface is not soft on the problem. He forcefully condemns it, and he has tried, with the establishment of a Vatican Commission to oversee policies on sexual abuse, to address the issue institutionally. At the same time, the preface shows that the path of mercy and forgiveness is what ultimately brings hope. This is exactly what Mr. Pittet describes in his own experience, which the pope affirms.

PRECEDENTS BEFORE POPE FRANCIS

Many discussions of mercy that I read during the Year of Mercy came across as if Pope Francis himself was almost the inventor of the theme. Overlooked, in my estimation, was the influence that Pope Saint John XXIII made on Francis's own thought. Most striking is the language that John XXIII used when he opened the Second Vatican Council. His opening address, *Gaudet Mater Ecclesia* ("Holy Mother Church Rejoices," October 11, 1962), which was largely ignored in its day but is now recognized as having given an orientation to the whole council, made two important references to mercy in his conception of what the ecumenical council was supposed to engender.

The first reference comes in the context of the admission of many highly problematic "errors" that one finds in the modern world and that keep cropping up. The pope then says,

> The Church has always opposed these errors. Frequently she has condemned them with the greatest severity. Nowadays however, the Spouse of Christ [that is, the Church] prefers to make use of the *medicine of mercy* rather than that of severity. She considers that she meets the needs of the present day by demonstrating the validity of her teaching rather than by condemnations. (*Gaudet Mater Ecclesia* 16)[3]

The emphasized phrase is striking. It evokes the image of mercy as a soothing balm, a medicine one takes when one is sick. The Church proffers this medicine freely to address the modern world's ills.

The second citation, only a few lines later in the address, speaks of the Church's desire to act in a tender and compassionate manner, like a mother toward her children. The pope says that the Church

> desires to show herself to be the loving mother of all, benign, patient, full of mercy and goodness toward those who are separated from her. To humanity, oppressed by so many difficulties, the Church says, as Peter said to the poor who begged alms from him: "I have neither gold nor silver, but what I have I give you; in the name of Jesus Christ of Nazareth, rise and walk" (Acts 3:6). In other words, the Church does not offer to the people of today riches that pass, nor does she promise them merely earthly happiness. But she distributes to them the goods of divine grace. (§17)

The pope then cites the importance of "Christian charity," which is unparalleled in "eradicating the seeds of discord, [with] nothing more efficacious in promoting concord, just peace, and the brotherly and sisterly unity of all."

In short, the pope's "pastoral" council was intended to reach out to wounded humanity—not just Catholics or Christians—to help bring about concord, peace, and justice into the world.

Pope Saint John Paul II's encyclical letter *Dives in Misericordia* ("Rich in Mercy," November 30, 1980) is a much longer document. It is inevitably much more detailed, offering both an extensive rehearsal of the biblical foundations of mercy and outlining the ways in which God's mercy, especially communicated in the person of Jesus Christ, impacts humanity today. The text is not easily summarized. All that we need do here, however, is point to several major ideas in the encyclical that touch our theme.

The first point to notice is the rationale the pope gives for issuing a message of mercy. Near the beginning of the text, he writes,

> The present-day mentality, more perhaps than that of people in the past, seems opposed to a God of mercy, and in fact tends to exclude from life and to remove from the human heart the very idea of mercy. The word and the concept of "mercy" seem to cause uneasiness in [humanity], who, thanks to the enormous development of science and technology, never before known in history, has become the master of the earth and has subdued and dominated it. (*DM* 2)

Even more forcefully, he adds that human beings today "need mercy even though they often do not realize it" (§2). People may not recognize the need for mercy, but the Church believes the message is nevertheless pertinent, and even urgent, in our modern context. That is why she raises a strong voice to draw attention to this widely ignored virtue.

A second insight comes from the encyclical's strongly christological orientation. Its focus is on Jesus Christ, who, as the revelation of the Father in heaven, presents a strong message of mercy, centered primarily on the cross and resurrection (*DM* 7). From a strictly Christian perspective, it is impossible to speak of God's mercy without referencing God's primary act of mercy in the gift of his only begotten Son to the world (John 3:16; Rom 5:8). Mercy is a *revealed* gift. The very beginning of the text draws upon the claim of Jesus in John's Gospel, "Whoever has seen me has seen the Father" (John 14:9; *DM* 1). Christ is where the true intersection of mercy and love meet. He is the mercy of God incarnate. He is pure love poured out for the world, light in the darkness. Pointing out the significance of the cross, the pope writes,

> In the eschatological fulfillment mercy will be revealed as love, while in the temporal phase, in human history, which is at the same time the history of sin and death, love must be revealed above all as mercy and must also be actualized as mercy. Christ's messianic program, the program of mercy, becomes the program of His people, the program of the Church. At its very center there is always the cross, for it is in the cross that the revelation of merciful love attains its culmination. (*DM* 8)

This citation shows that there is an end goal in mind. Mercy moves us toward the kingdom of God, where pure love and mercy will be perpetual. From a Christian perspective, one cannot simply exhort human beings to mercy. We must proclaim the mercy that has already been shown the world, and then invite everyone to partake of it and to share it. Moreover, the text carries the argument one step further by emphasizing that the message of mercy embodied in love shows that love is stronger than death, and that love is more powerful than evil (§8).

Another insight from this encyclical is the use of the parable of the prodigal son as a primary biblical analogy for mercy (§5). Without a doubt, it is a well-known and beloved parable. (It has inspired many artists throughout history to illustrate out, such as Rembrandt, Guercino, Murillo, Bassano, Tissot, etc.) Pointing out the strong connection between the Lukan tradition of mercy, which we examined in chapter 4, and the Old Testament, the pope presents an extensive explanation of Jesus' teaching on mercy using this parable. He particularly draws attention to the younger son's coming to his senses, realizing his sinfulness, and intending to come to his father in a most humble way. Rather than being punished for his rash running off and squandering his inheritance (even before his father's death), he finds a merciful father awaiting him, welcoming him back with open arms. Undeserved mercy shows how love overcomes our weaknesses and failings.

The encyclical adds another layer to the gift of divine mercy by offering Mary, the mother of Jesus, as a model for mercy (§9). This is unsurprising, given John Paul II's intense devotion to the Blessed Virgin Mary. He regularly invokes her in his teachings, and it is present here. She is honored as one who exceptionally received God's mercy through her immaculate conception, but also through her bearing of the Word-made-flesh, Jesus Christ. Additionally, she is the one whose great hymn, the Magnificat (Luke 1:46–55), that we saw in chapter 4, speaks of God's "mercy…from generation to generation." Mary thus becomes an intergenerational figure, we might say, one who calls each generation to remember the mercy of God (*DM* 10).

The language of "generations" leads the pope to analyze, at some length, the anxieties and problems of the modern world, "this generation" (§§10–12). Many of the huge challenges faced in the modern world make him wonder whether justice can ever be enough. The challenges are, in fact, almost overwhelming. One cannot simply restore balance in life by pursuing justice alone. There must be room for mercy. This is the thrust of the entire document. The Church stands by its mission to share God's mercy (§13). Because she herself has received mercy, so she is called to extend it to others. Quoting Jesus' teaching in the Sermon on the Mount about the merciful being "blessed" (Matt 5:7), the encyclical strongly affirms the desire of the Church to "put mercy into practice" (*DM* 14).

It is worth adding, here, another perspective from Vatican Council II itself. When speaking of the ministry of the laity in the Decree on the Apostolate of the Laity, the council teaches,

> Since the works of charity and mercy express the most striking testimony of the Christian life, apostolic formation should lead also to the performance of these works so that the faithful may learn from childhood on to have compassion for their brethren and to be generous in helping those in need. (*Apostolicam Actuositatem*, "Apostolic Activity," November 18, 1965, §31c)

In a sense, John Paul's encyclical simply reinforces the conciliar goal: Christians must perform acts of charity and mercy because they are the most concrete signs that God is still reaching out to sinful humanity and bringing about healing and reconciliation.

So here we have a digest of a major encyclical letter outlining the Church's approach to mercy and why it is needed in the world today. We have not done justice to the full teaching, certainly. The document uses the word *mercy* (in the English translation) nearly 220 times! Other synonyms, such as *compassion* and *love*, appear as well. But the heart of the teaching is solid. God is rich in mercy, and so should we be.

CLOSING ONE DOOR AND OPENING ANOTHER

Another Church document to consider is Pope Francis's own apostolic letter issued at the end of the Year of Mercy, *Misericordia et Misera*. It is a brief text in comparison to the encyclicals we have examined. It nevertheless outlines the pope's vision of a more merciful Church moving forward toward the kingdom of God.

The text opens with a beautiful image taken from Saint Augustine's description of Jesus' moving encounter with the woman taken in adultery (John 8:1–11). After the woman's accusers drift away one by one in light of Jesus' challenge to let the one without sin cast the first stone, Augustine poignantly comments, "The two of them alone remained: *mercy with misery*" (*MM* 1). Augustine's phrase in Latin gives the apostolic letter its title, *Misericordia et Misera*. The way the pope sees it, mercy stands alongside misery and is the proper response to it.

Five points in Pope Francis's apostolic letter are particularly pertinent.[4] The first is the concreteness of the pope's vision. Mercy is tied to many different actions. He particularly emphasizes its relationship to forgiveness. For instance, he writes,

> *Forgiveness* is the most visible sign of the Father's love, which Jesus sought to reveal by his entire life. Every page of the Gospel is marked by this imperative of a love that loves to the point of forgiveness. Even at the last moment of his earthly life, as he was being nailed to the cross, Jesus spoke words of forgiveness: "Father, forgive them; for they know not what they do" (*Lk* 23:34). (§2)

Catholics, of course, will inevitably tie this forgiveness to the sacrament of reconciliation (penance). So, it is not surprising that the pope underlines the importance of regular reception of the sacrament (§8). He also strongly encourages priests to be merciful within the sacrament, something he emphasized in earlier teachings (§10). In addition to the sacrament of reconciliation, other concrete gestures are encouraged, especially participation in the Eucharist and good catechesis. He basically urges people "to *celebrate* mercy" (§5).

A second point is an explicit connection the pope makes between mercy and consolation. Although we have not examined the language of consolation explicitly regarding mercy in the Bible, the point is well made. Comfort or consolation goes hand in hand with mercy. It helps people cope with their suffering. The pope writes,

> Another face of mercy is *consolation*. "Comfort, comfort my people" (Is 40:1) is the heartfelt plea that the

> prophet continues to make today, so that a word of hope may come to all those who experience suffering and pain. (§13)

A third point of the document touches the very purpose of this book. Pope Francis emphasizes the importance of reading the Bible, the Word of God, as a valuable resource for comprehending the biblical and ecclesial teaching on mercy. He says,

> The *Bible* is the great story of the marvels of God's mercy. Every one of its pages is steeped in the love of the Father who from the moment of creation wished to impress the signs of his love on the universe....I greatly desire that God's word be increasingly celebrated, known and disseminated, so that the mystery of love streaming from this font of mercy may be ever better understood. (§7)

These words dovetail nicely with the Second Vatican Council's call for better dissemination of the Word of God (*Dei Verbum* 26). The pope also invites priests to preach good homilies on the Word, while encouraging all the faithful to listen carefully to the Word of God, to *hear* it well (*MM* 6). The goal of this book, in fact, has been to help fulfill this ideal.

A fourth teaching in the document is the demand to cultivate a "culture of mercy." He explicitly states,

> We are called to promote a *culture of mercy* based on the rediscovery of encounter with others, a culture in which no one looks at another with indifference or turns away from the suffering of our brothers and sisters. *The works of mercy are "handcrafted,"* in the sense that none of them is alike. Our hands can craft them in a thousand different ways, and even though the one God inspires

> them, and they are all fashioned from the same "material," mercy itself, each one takes on a different form. (§20)

Notice that this passage employs the concrete image of the uniqueness of each gesture of mercy. They are like fine handcrafts, each one designed for a special purpose and achieving a specific goal. To promote such a "culture of mercy" is not easy in an environment where an attitude of judgment seems to prevail. The perspective of human justice is not sufficient. Divine justice calls upon mercy.

Finally, the document leaves its discussion of mercy somewhat open-ended. Recall that during the Year of Mercy (as with other jubilee years), the central door of St. Peter's Basilica in Rome—called the "holy door"—was left open throughout the year for pilgrims to walk through as part of their participation in prayerful activities. (The pope invited cathedrals and other churches or shrines through the world to do the same.) At the end of the year, the pope formally closed the door; it will not be opened until another holy year is proclaimed. But the pope's final teaching employs the image of the door in a novel way: "The Jubilee now ends and the Holy Door is closed. But the door of mercy of our heart continues to remain wide open" (*MM* 16). That is indeed the most crucial point. The door of mercy in our hearts is supposed to remain open. Otherwise the message of mercy will seem only fleeting, temporary, transitional, and not life-changing. So the pope's message essentially calls on the faithful to leave their merciful hearts ajar. It is this openness that alone can encourage the free reception and sharing of the most precious gift of mercy.

These five points cannot express the totality of Pope Francis's teaching. But they do impart the flavor of it and indicate some of its importance. It was intended as an ongoing message. Just as the biblical refrain insists that God's mercy is everlasting (Ps 118), so is the Holy Father's plea for the Church and the world to become a more hospitable place for God's mercy to lodge. Pope Francis has enunciated the vision clearly. The rest will be up to the Church, and to us, to implement it.

MERCY FROM AN INTERNATIONAL PERSPECTIVE

I would be remiss to ignore one of the thornier questions of modern life that touches our theme of mercy, namely, an ecclesial perspective on the issue of war. This is one of the most vexing ongoing issues in human existence. While I don't wish to go too far afield in an area that requires its own special study, we can at least draw attention to how such an issue resonates with the theme of mercy and relates to social justice. Most of this book has obviously been oriented to personal and communal dimensions of mercy. There is also, however, an international dimension worth recalling. It involves relations between nations. Once more, the topic is much larger than can be addressed here. It is a theme that relates more to moral theology than to a biblical study, as such. But one can legitimately ask, "What role does mercy play on an international level?" The question is even more pertinent because the Bible, especially the Old Testament, as we noted in chapter 2, recounts many instances of wars.

Scholars have often noted that Vatican Council II was famous for not pronouncing any anathemas (from the Greek word for "let it be accursed"). What is sometimes overlooked, however, is that the council strongly condemned the nuclear arms race (*GS* 81). The council says, "The arms race is an utterly treacherous trap for humanity, and one which ensnares the poor to an intolerable degree." It also unequivocally condemns indiscriminate wars:

> Any act of war aimed indiscriminately at the destruction of entire cities of extensive areas along with their population is a crime against God and man himself. It merits unequivocal and unhesitating condemnation. (§80; see also CCC §2314)

We no longer live in the Middle Ages, when wars were conducted, albeit brutally, with swords, scabbards, bows and arrows, and the like. Already with the two great World Wars and almost countless other armed conflicts, humanity has witnessed the potential destruction that modern warfare can wreak. We have also seen atrocious acts of genocide and the terrible consequences of hatred. The reason the Church so strongly condemns nuclear armament and calls for the avoidance of war is that the potential for total annihilation of the human race has never been so evident. One only has to think of the horrors of Nagasaki and Hiroshima to realize the scope of possible destruction that modern nuclear war could unleash. And modern nuclear arms are multiple times more destructive than those used near the end of World War II. The *Catechism* teaches that nations should do everything possible to avoid warfare (§§ 2307–14), while acknowledging the complexity of situations that can exist in international relations.

It is true that the Catholic Church has traditionally recognized the possibility of a "just war," based upon principles laid out in the Middle Ages by Saint Thomas Aquinas (see CCC §2309), first enunciated in the fourth century by Saint Augustine.[5] But this theory, based upon a theory of natural law, was always understood within severe constraints of certain criteria that had to be met to justify a war. Unfortunately, all too often, the criteria have been used to rationalize war rather than work through the required steps to determine whether a war is truly just. Many theologians, and modern popes, now think that modern circumstances make such a just war almost impossible, given the possibility of mass destruction that is now possible through scientific advances of nuclear and chemical weapons. In fact, a landmark conference at the Vatican held in the spring of 2016 basically called into question the contemporary viability of the just war theory, considering modern circumstances and biblical teachings, especially the radical call of Jesus for love of enemies. Pope Francis strongly supported the conclusions of the conference, which were announced by Cardinal Peter

Turkson, the head of a new dicastery (Vatican office) established by Pope Francis to address issues of human development, justice, peace, healthcare, and migration.[6] There has also been speculation that Pope Francis may well prepare an encyclical on the topic of war and peace, something John XXIII did in 1963 with the publication of *Pacem in Terris* ("Peace on Earth"), a document that remains as timely as ever.

We might recall, here, how a biblical perspective lends support for this pacifist perspective. Although war was a frequent problem in the ancient world and throughout Israel's history, there is also a strain of pacifism that can be found in the Bible. Even the Old Testament bears witness to this attitude. The prophet Micah, for instance, offers an idealistic vision of the day when the nations assemble before God on the highest of the mountains to be instructed in the Lord's ways. Then he announces,

> He [God] shall judge between many peoples, / and shall arbitrate between strong nations far away; / they shall beat their swords into plowshares, / and their spears into pruning hooks; / nation shall not lift up sword against nation, / neither shall they learn war any more; / but they shall all sit under their own vines and under their own fig trees, / and no one shall make them afraid; / for the mouth of the Lord of hosts has spoken. (Mic 4:3–4; see also Isa 2:2–4)

This vision is eschatological (oriented toward the end-time), to be sure, but it also indicates the Lord's preference. All nations should strive toward harmony and avoid war.

The New Testament vision is even more demanding. Jesus clearly taught an alternative to violence, war, and hatred. The Sermon on the Mount's "antitheses"—so called because they radicalize or even abrogate parts of the Old Testament Torah—provide the basic orientation. Jesus teaches,

> You have heard that it was said to those of ancient times, "You shall not murder"; and "whoever murders shall be liable to judgment." But I say to you that if you are angry with a brother or sister, you will be liable to judgment; and if you insult a brother or sister, you will be liable to the council; and if you say, "You fool," you will be liable to the hell of fire. (Matt 5:21–22)

> You have heard that it was said, "An eye for an eye and a tooth for a tooth." But I say to you, Do not resist an evildoer. But if anyone strikes you on the right cheek, turn the other also. (Matt 5:38–39)

> You have heard that it was said, "You shall love your neighbor and hate your enemy." But I say to you, Love your enemies and pray for those who persecute you. (Matt 5:43–44)

These teachings have always been difficult to put into practice. From Matthew's perspective, they are part of the radical call of Jesus for his disciples to observe the "greater righteousness" (Matt 5:20, au. trans.). In other words, the way for Jesus' disciples is the road of mercy and forgiveness rather than the path of war. Some Christian groups (e.g., Quakers, Amish) have historically tried to live out these values literally, but most of the time, Christians bemoan how impossible such values seem in the midst of everyday life. Exceptions, of course, have always existed. One thinks of Francis of Assisi, for instance, or in more modern times, Dorothy Day or Thomas Merton. Merton, in fact, has a powerful quotation that is pertinent here:

> The beginning of the fight against hatred, the basic Christian answer to hatred, is not the commandment to love, but what must necessarily come before in order

> to make the commandment bearable and comprehensible. It is a prior commandment, *to believe*. The root of Christian love is not the will to love, but *the faith that one is loved*. The faith that one is loved by God although unworthy—or, rather, irrespective of one's worth!
>
> In the true Christian vision of God's love, the idea of worthiness loses its significance. Revelation of the mercy of God makes the whole problem of worthiness something almost laughable: the discovery that worthiness is of no special consequence (since no one could ever, by himself, be strictly worthy to be loved with such a love) is a true liberation of the spirit. And until this discovery is made, until this liberation has been brought about by the divine mercy, man [*sic*] is imprisoned in hate.[7]

Note, here, how Merton draws attention to God's initiative. God is the Merciful One, the Loving One. Only once we have grasped this, and are open to accepting that undeserved love, will we be truly capable of showing mercy to others. So the challenge remains.

Even on the international level, then, the Church calls for restraint when it comes to protectionism and nationalism. While the Church rightly recognizes the legitimacy of self-defense, the potential for outright destruction in our age calls for far more finesse when reacting to real or perceived threats to national security. Violence and war should not be the first reaction. Diplomacy should be exercised, and nations should attempt to seek ways constructively and peaceably to resolve their differences. This advice may not fall literally under the rubric of "mercy," but it issues from the same source and leads in the same direction.

CONCLUSION

With these two brief summaries of the biblical and ecclesial teaching on mercy, we come to the end of our project. Hopefully it is evident now that mercy is not an option. Mercy really matters as much today as it ever did. It is in God's very nature to be merciful to us human beings. But it is also something that we, in imitation of divine mercy, should be willing to impart to others.

REFLECTION QUESTIONS

1. Do you think Pope Francis's vision calling for a more merciful and compassionate Church is realistic? Is it fair? Are there limits to such a vision?
2. How do you think being merciful and not promoting more sinfulness can be held in balance? In its teaching on mercy, does the Bible inadvertently promote laxity in the moral life? Why or why not?
3. Do you think mercy and love trump power and might? What is the relationship between justice and mercy in the modern world?
4. Do you think mercy can change people's hearts? What role can mercy and compassion play in a world filled with violence, crime, hatred, terrorism, and war?
5. How would you relate the Bible's teaching on mercy to the Catholic Church's teachings on this theme? How does the teaching of Pope Francis on mercy compare with previous Church teachings on the theme?

NOTES

INTRODUCTION

1. For an explanation of the Church's teaching on indulgences, see the *Catechism* (CCC) §1471.

2. The pope's choice of the date was not unreasonable. Although no one knows the precise date of Saint Paul's birth, scholars propose a range between 1 and 10 CE.

3. For more information, see Ronald D. Witherup, *Saint Paul and the New Evangelization* (Collegeville: Liturgical Press, 2013).

CHAPTER 1: THE LANGUAGE OF MERCY

1. David Noel Freedman, et al., eds., *The Anchor Bible Dictionary*, 6 vols. (New York/London: Doubleday, 1992), 4:699.

2. *Merriam-Webster's Collegiate Dictionary*, 11th. ed. (Springfield, MA: Merriam-Webster, 2007), 776.

3. John L. McKenzie, *Dictionary of the Bible* (New York: Macmillan, 1965), 565.

4. Walter Kasper, *Mercy: The Essence of the Gospel and the Key to Christian Life* (New York: Paulist Press, 2014).

5. See http://w2.vatican.va/content/francesco/en/angelus/2013/documents/papa-francesco_angelus_20130317.html (accessed March 28, 2017).

6. Cardinal Walter Kasper, *Pope Francis' Revolution of Tenderness and Love: Theological and Pastoral Perspectives* (New York: Paulist Press, 2016).

7. Such passages in the Gospels are not anti-Pharisee or anti-Jewish, as such. They give witness to a time when Christians were separating, or had separated, from Judaism, and tensions between the two groups grew. Such passages remind us of the danger of inflexible, arrogant, and overly self-assured religious attitudes in any era and by any faith.

CHAPTER 2: IS GOD *REALLY* MERCIFUL? AN OLD TESTAMENT PERSPECTIVE

1. For an orientation to these issues, see Thomas Römer, *Dark God: Cruelty, Sex, and Violence in the Old Testament* (Mahwah, NJ: Paulist Press, 2013); Jerome F. D. Creach, *Violence in Scripture* (Louisville: Westminster John Knox Press, 2013); and Eric A. Seibert, *The Violence of Scripture: Overcoming the Old Testament's Troubling Legacy* (Minneapolis, MN: Fortress Press, 2012).

2. A good, concise explanation of the issue of violence in the Bible can be found in the Pontifical Biblical Commission document, *The Inspiration and Truth of Sacred Scripture* (Collegeville, MN: Liturgical Press, 2014), §§124–31.

3. Labeling these stories "myths" is not a denial of the truth they contain. Myth is not falsehood. Myth is a literary genre of storytelling that addresses deep truths, such as birth, death, love, creation, evil, and so on. The Church recognizes that the Genesis stories are not necessarily literally, historically true in their details. Rather, they speak to the deep purpose of God's creation. See the Pontifical Biblical Commission's 1993 document, *The Interpretation of the Bible in the Church*, §III.C.4, which speaks of "the language of myth" in some parts of the Bible.

4. The expression comes from Professor John R. Donahue, to whom I am grateful.

5. After the golden age of King David and King Solomon, "Israel" was split into two kingdoms (ca. 922 BCE). Israel was the northern kingdom and Judah the southern. If I use "Israel" somewhat inaccurately at times, it is for the sake of simplification. In this book, the expression "people of Israel" represents the entire

Jewish people, the people of the covenant, and not necessarily the residents of the northern kingdom.

6. I let the masculine term remain here because, in fact, most prophets in the Old Testament were male. We should recall that there were female prophets (prophetesses), such as Deborah (Judg 4:4) or Huldah (2 Kgs 22:14; 2 Chr 34:22), but they have not left any written testimony, unlike their male counterparts whose books are in the Bible.

7. For more information on social justice in the Bible, see the excellent resource of John R. Donahue, *Seek Justice That You May Live: Reflections and Resources on the Bible and Social Justice* (Mahwah, NJ: Paulist Press, 2014).

CHAPTER 3: JESUS, THE "FACE OF THE FATHER'S MERCY": A NEW TESTAMENT PERSPECTIVE

1. Caspar Milquetoast was a 1920s cartoon figure, the essence of the meek, nonassertive, overly timid individual. The name slid into the English language as a sobriquet for a person lacking "backbone."

2. The phrase can also be translated "seventy times seven times," making the gesture even more grandiose.

3. For a good explanation of the importance of the resurrection, see Frank J. Matera, *Resurrection: The Origin and Goal of the Christian Life* (Collegeville, MN: Liturgical Press, 2015).

4. See Francis J. Moloney, *Love in the Gospel of John: An Exegetical, Theological, and Literary Study* (Grand Rapids, MI: Baker Academic, 2013).

CHAPTER 4: LUKE, THE GOSPEL OF MERCY

1. The image is found in the Catacomb of Callixtus in Rome, along the Appian Way, and dates from the middle of the third century CE. In addition to the Gospel of John (10:11–18), the shepherd image for Jesus is found in Hebrews 13:20; 1 Peter 2:25; 5:4 (cf. Matt 2:6; Mark 6:34). Psalm 23, which portrays God as a

benign shepherd, may also provide some of the background for this image. In Ezekiel, God also promises to be the one true shepherd for his people (34:15–16).

2. A drachma was a Greek coin, equivalent to a Roman denarius, worth a typical day's wage.

3. Some ancient manuscripts are missing this line, but it is entirely consistent with Lucan theology.

CHAPTER 5: SAINT PAUL AND THE MERCY OF GOD

1. The phrase in italics literally is a divine passive: "as we have been shown mercy" (Gk. *ēleēthēmen*). The NABRE translates, "through the mercy shown us," which preserves both the passive sense and the instrumental idea.

2. This passage contains a list of important Christian virtues, of which one is "tenderheartedness" or "a heart of mercy" (NET) or "heartfelt compassion" (NABRE), which the NRSV translates somewhat limply as "compassion." The Greek (*splangchna oiktirmou*) expresses deep emotion.

CHAPTER 6: SAINT PAUL REVISITED: MISPERCEPTIONS ABOUT MERCY?

1. The entire topic of homosexuality in the Bible is very complex. While I would not agree with every interpretation offered in the following two resources, they provide a useful introduction to the question: Innocent Himbaza, Adrien Schenker, and Jean-Baptiste Edart, *The Bible on the Question of Homosexuality*, trans. Benedict M. Guevin (Washington, DC: The Catholic University of America Press, 2012); and Louis J. Cameli, *Catholic Teaching on Homosexuality: New Paths to Understanding* (Notre Dame, IN: Ave Maria Press, 2012). Apart from questions of morality, the *Catechism* calls on Catholics to be pastorally sensitive and to treat persons of homosexual orientation with the "respect, compassion, and sensitivity" owed to all human beings (CCC §2358). The virulent reaction on the part of some ultra-rightist "Catholic" social media sites in

mid-2017 to James Martin's short, pastorally oriented book, *Building a Bridge: How the Catholic Church and the LGBT Community Can Enter into a Relationship of Respect, Compassion, and Sensitivity* (San Francisco: HarperOne, 2017) shows just how difficult it is to implement the biblical teaching of mercy when it comes to a "hot button" topic like homosexuality.

2. Note that the Pontifical Biblical Commission's recent document on inspiration, using Paul's view of women's roles in the Church, warns against exaggerating limited cultural perspectives found in the Bible. They write, "We must not confuse the principles and their application, which is always determined by the social and cultural context." See *The Inspiration and Truth of Sacred Scripture*, §133.

CHAPTER 7: MERCY IN THE CHURCH AND IN THE MODERN WORLD

1. The title is taken from the Canticle of the Creatures composed by Saint Francis of Assisi (ca. 1181–1226) in praise of all creation.

2. Vatican Radio reported this story on February 13, 2017, and several news services picked it up.

3. I have adapted slightly the translation of the quotations from *Gaudet Mater Ecclesia* to make them more inclusive.

4. Emphases (italics) in the citations that follow are from the original document.

5. See the *Compendium of the Social Doctrine of the Church* (Città del Vaticano: Libreria Editrice Vaticana, 2004), §§500–501, accessed February 23, 2017, https://web.archive.org/web/20160802175343/http://www.vatican.va/roman_curia/pontifical_councils/justpeace/documents/rc_pc_justpeace_doc_20060526_compendio-dott-soc_en.html. An excellent treatment of war and peace in the Christian tradition is Lisa Sowle Cahill, *Love Your Enemies: Discipleship, Pacifism, and Just War Theory* (Minneapolis, MN: Fortress Press, 1994).

6. See Joshua J. McElwee, "Cardinal Turkson: 'We Do Not Stop War by Starting Another War,'" *NCR*, September 20, 2016, https://www.ncronline.org/news/people/cardinal-turkson-we-do-not-stop-war-starting-another-war.

7. Thomas Merton, *New Seeds of Contemplation* (New York: New Directions Publishing, 1961), 74–75, emphases in the original.

FOR FURTHER READING

The Bible Today 55, no. 4 (July/August 2017). Published by Liturgical Press, this issue on the Bible is devoted entirely to "The Mercy of God."

Janus, Mark-David, ed. *Crossing the Threshold of Mercy: A Spiritual Guide for the Extraordinary Jubilee Year of Mercy*. New York: Paulist Press, 2015. A useful compendium of materials proposed for use throughout the Year of Mercy. It remains a useful guide to continue reflections on the theme.

Kasper, Walter. *Mercy: The Essence of the Gospel and the Key to Christian Life*. New York: Paulist Press, 2014. A sophisticated theological explanation of the theme of mercy in Christianity by a renowned German theologian and cardinal, which began as a series of conferences for a papal retreat and inspired Pope Francis to call the Church to greater mercy.

———. *Pope Francis' Revolution of Tenderness and Love: Theological and Pastoral Perspectives*. New York: Paulist Press, 2016. An explanation of the motives and impact of Pope Francis's vision for the reform of the Church through the gospel message of mercy.

Keenan, James F. *The Works of Mercy: The Heart of Catholicism*. 3rd ed. Lanham, MD: Rowman and Littlefield, 2017. An excellent overview of the role of the works of mercy in the Catholic tradition written by a moral theologian. This edition updates resources and adds new material, including a chapter on

Pope Francis and one on Abraham Lincoln's proclamation of Thanksgiving and its contemporary pertinence.

Pontifical Council for the Promotion of the New Evangelization. *Celebrating Mercy*. Huntington, IN: Our Sunday Visitor, 2015. The official text from the Holy See explaining many aspects of the Year of Mercy.

———. *Mercy in the Fathers of the Church*. Huntington, IN: Our Sunday Visitor, 2015. A resource published for the Year of Mercy and citing many passages from the early Church Fathers on the theme of mercy.

———. *Mercy in the Teaching of the Popes*. Huntington, IN: Our Sunday Visitor, 2015. A compendium of papal teachings on the theme of mercy, intended as a resource for reflection throughout the Year of Mercy.

———. *The Parables of Mercy*. Huntington, IN: Our Sunday Visitor, 2015. An explanation of the parables of Jesus that address the theme of mercy in the New Testament.

———. *The Psalms of Mercy*. Huntington, IN: Our Sunday Visitor, 2015. Another resource for the Year of Mercy from the Holy See that contains reflections on ten psalms of mercy in the Old Testament (Pss 25; 41—43; 51; 57; 92; 103; 119:81–88; and 136).

———. *The Saints in Mercy*. Huntington, IN: Our Sunday Visitor, 2015. Another resource for the Year of Mercy published by the Holy See and containing examples of mercy among the saints.

Pope Francis. *The Church of Mercy: A Vision for the Church*. Chicago: Loyola Press, 2014. A compilation of Pope Francis's essays, homilies, and allocutions that demonstrate the breadth of his vision for the Church, which embraces the poor and calls for mercy.

———. *Misericordia et Misera* ("Mercy and Misery"). Vatican City: Libreria Editrice Vaticana, 2016. Accessed February 11, 2017. https://w2.vatican.va/content/francesco/en/apost_letters/documents/papa-francesco-lettera-ap_20161120_misericordia-et-misera.html. Apostolic Letter issued at the close of the Year of Mercy (November 2016) to call people to a "culture of mercy."

———. *Misericordiae Vultus* ("The Face of Mercy"). Vatican City: Libreria Editrice Vaticana, 2015. Accessed February 11, 2017. http://w2.vatican.va/content/francesco/en/apost_letters/documents/papa-francesco_bolla_20150411_misericordiae-vultus.html. The papal bull that promulgated the Extraordinary Jubilee Year of Mercy and outlined the pope's basic approach to the theme of mercy.

———. *The Name of God Is Mercy: A Conversation with Andrea Tornielli*. New York: Random House, 2016. A published interview with Pope Francis that candidly shows the Pope's orientation toward a more merciful Church.

Pope John Paul II. *Dives in Misericordia* ("On the Mercy of God"). Vatican City: Libreria Editrice Vaticana, 1980. Accessed February 11, 2017. http://w2.vatican.va/content/john-paul-ii/en/encyclicals/documents/hf_jp-ii_enc_30111980_dives-in-misericordia.html. An encyclical letter (November 1980) with a good section digesting much of the Old Testament teaching on mercy. It also made the parable of the prodigal son the virtual icon of mercy from the New Testament.

Schönborn, Christophe. *We Have Found Mercy: The Mystery of Divine Mercy*. Edited by Hubert Philipp Weber. San Francisco: Ignatius Press, 2012. Focusing on Pope (Saint) John Paul II as the "pope of mercy," this is a series of reflections from a noted German theologian and cardinal who became a leading spokesman for Pope Francis.